BOOM LIFE

A Guide to Life-Enhancement

HEALTH   ENVIRONMENT   CAREER

FINANCES   SOCIAL/FUN   FAMILY

INTIMACY   SPIRITUALITY

MICHELLE B. CURRIE, MA

BALBOA.
PRESS

A DIVISION OF HAY HOUSE

Balboa Press books may be ordered through booksellers or by contacting:

Balboa Press
A Division of Hay House
1663 Liberty Drive
Bloomington, IN 47403
www.balboapress.com
1 (877) 407-4847

Print information available on the last page.

ISBN: 978-1-5043-4358-9 (sc)
ISBN: 978-1-5043-4360-2 (hc)
ISBN: 978-1-5043-4359-6 (e)

Library of Congress Control Number: 2015917662

Balboa Press rev. date: 11/05/2015

Disclaimer

There are lots and lots of client stories throughout this workbook. I have changed names and combined elements of client stories to respect confidentiality. So, if you know me, or have worked with me, you might see an element or two of your story within this workbook but you will see that it is not exactly your story The stories about me are mine and true to my memory of them.

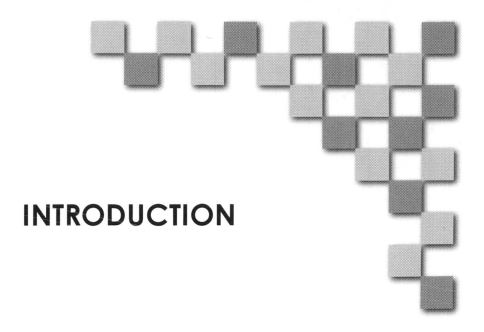

INTRODUCTION

It wasn't until I was divorced for the second time that I stopped reacting to my life and started being proactive. What does that mean? Well, I began to look at the different areas of my life and to determine how happy I was with them and then set goals and action steps to make changes. I was very, very tired of life happening to me. I was ready to make my life happen! Like a "boom economy" I needed a "boom life."

When I told my parents that I was separated and would be getting a second divorce, my Dad, Conrad, said these fateful words: "Now Michelle, don't hide get on your bike, keep your head up, keep your balance and ride throughout your life." By this time I was dating my soon-to-be third husband, Bob, and his response to my father was that he was going to ride right next to me and maybe put engines on both bikes. That was in 1990 and it has been a great ride and we are looking forward to more bike riding.

I liked the visual of getting on a bike and riding it through my life. I would be the navigator. I would be responsible for keeping the tires pumped. I would have to keep moving to have balance and balance is key. I have used this analogy ever since to examine my own life every year, to make sure that my tires are strong enough to carry me where I want to go. I check my balance to be sure that I can ride my bike (my life) with as much ease as possible and when the terrain gets rough I can manage that as well with a strong set of wheels and excellent balance.

I invite you to get on your bike, but first you need to check your tires to make sure they are not flat, that you have enough spokes, and that you have balance. This workbook is meant to help you have fun with the ride that is your life. In the process, you will enhance your life and the lives of others around you.

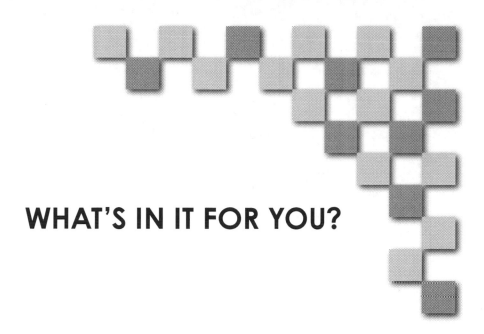

WHAT'S IN IT FOR YOU?

My work as a business consultant and coach for the past twenty-five plus years has brought me in contact with hundreds of business people. Most of my clients work in privately owned businesses selling and servicing industrial machinery such as construction equipment, agricultural equipment, pumps, compressors, material handling equipment, commercial tires, and on and on. The respect I have for the leaders/owners/managers of these businesses is tremendous. My interactions with these men (yes, by far at least ninety-eight percent are men) range from operational (how to run their businesses) to personal (how their lives are functioning).

I have also provided life coaching to many people throughout the years. While my business consulting and coaching has been with men, my life coaching experiences have been mostly with women. These experiences have put me in the unique position of being privy to the personal ups and downs of all these people. So, whether you are a business person, stay-at-home man or woman, the strategies and structures of this workbook will assist you in enhancing your life.

Let's look at an example.

John's Lack of Balance

John pulled me aside at a meeting so that we could speak away from the others in the group. He said that his wife was unhappy with his focus on the business to the detriment of their relationship. He knew that he had lost touch with his children and couldn't tell me much about their high school years. He was proud of his accomplishments at work and was confused because he felt that providing financial security for his family was his reason for being. He asked me what he should do.

Because John felt he was the key element to the continued success of his company, he feared relinquishing control of his business. He demanded that his executive team and his managers put in the same amount of time, energy, and commitment that he did. Now he was beginning to understand that a large contributor to the turnover in personnel was due to a culture that equated long hours with good performance which led to a lack of life balance for his employees.

John began to examine his life using the Boom Life methodology and it became very clear that he lacked satisfaction in several areas of his life. Adjustments were difficult but he made them and these adjustments lead to better relationships with his wife, his family, his friends, and his staff.

John is not alone, everyone needs to take stock of what is happening to the entire landscape of their lives at least once a year and make adjustments to areas that are "out of balance." Why? The answer is very personal to each individual; but for the most part, this issue of balance enhances your life: it brings on a Boom Life!

Riding Your Bike

Albert Einstein said it best: "Life is like riding a bicycle. To keep your balance you have to keep moving." Welcome to your bicycle/life-enhancement. You may have tried to make life improvements in the past without much success. Even though you feel capable, you may struggle to figure out how to truly change or what to change. This comprehensive program will help you pinpoint how your limiting thoughts and beliefs are currently blocking your progress. Through a series of questions and visualizations, you will begin to ignite the profound changes you've been craving in each area of your life.

What does it take to ride your bike through your life? Well you will need a good set of wheels. If you prefer a unicycle, it will be one big wheel. If you prefer a more traditional bicycle, it will need two wheels. As you get older you may trade your bike in for an adult tricycle. No matter how many wheels you have you will have to check those wheels for leaks, weaknesses, nails, and the like. You also have to keep moving, in other words you have to get up and out and live your life. Without movement you lose your balance and will fall off your bike. It is simply all the areas of your life that work together as a system. I have found eight major life areas that make up the wheel. In no particular order these areas are:

Health - Environment - Finances - Career - Family - Social/Fun – Intimate Relationship - Spirituality.

Look at these eight life elements as spokes on your wheels. If one spoke is smaller than the others the wheel will not run efficiently. If there are several areas that are "off" then the wheel may not roll at all. The reality is that some of you may not have one of the life areas above. For instance, if you are retired or have enough money that you do not need to work – congratulations; you may not have the Career spoke. But the other areas of your life are there, so instead of wheels with eight spokes, you have seven. You might add a life area which is important to you which is great. What you can't do is eliminate too many life sections because the strength of your wheels will become compromised the fewer spokes you have. The rounder the tires and the more you are proactive, the more balance and satisfaction with life and the easier it is to ride that bike.

BALANCE

It is important to understand how the concept of "balance" is used here. At first blush, you might think of time as the balance element. If this were the case then to have balance you would have to put an equal amount of time into each of the eight life elements. This is not practical or achievable.

When I speak of balance I am measuring the amount of satisfaction a person has in each of the eight life elements as well as the activity of life itself. As you dig into this workbook I will guide you to examine each of the eight life elements and determine your level of satisfaction with each one. The act of completing this workbook (especially on a yearly basis) will provide the momentum you need to maintain your balance.

To achieve balance we are looking for satisfaction ratings in all eight areas that are within one point of each other. A satisfied life will have ratings in the four to five range. Now, if your ratings are all low - two or below - you do not have a balanced life because balance is about satisfaction and happiness, you need to work to lift up each life area.

My Story

Every year for the past twenty-five plus years I have completed what I consider to be a life audit. I look at the eight life areas and rate each one as to how satisfied I am with it and then work on the areas that are out of whack.

In the year 2000, I found that my satisfaction with my career was lower than I expected. It was to the point that I had lost some of my motivation. After reflecting on my career, I realized that to improve my satisfaction I would need to go back to school. I wanted to focus more on the psychological and behavioral side of running a business. I wanted my Master's degree. But how could I do this? I was working full time and traveling; my time with family and friends was stretched already; I was involved in two non-profit organizations (on their Board of Directors); and more.

How did I do it? I looked to the other seven areas of my life and asked them to give a little for the next few years and it worked. I kept up my health regimen. I asked family and friends to be patient with me while I focused on my studies. I talked to my husband about my decision and he got on board quickly. I asked for a partial leave of absence from work and everyone agreed. My husband was willing to take on more of the financial burden in the short term for the long-term rewards. I set up areas in my home and at work to make it easier to study. And I certainly prayed that I had what it took to get through. I graduated with my MA in Counseling Psychology in 2003: no small feat, but it is one that is paying off for me personally and in business.

As you can see, if another area in my life was out of whack - or worse, two or three areas - getting my degree would have been much more difficult. Family would have resented my time away from them; friends might not have been patient with me, which would not have made the goal impossible, but certainly more difficult.

Balance allows you to cope with whatever life has in store for you. While you never know what's around the corner, you are far more equipped to deal with setbacks when you have a firm understanding of your life. You may attain perfect balance, but then the unexpected happens. You lose your job. Your spouse dies. These events are somewhat out of your control but if you have a good understanding of your life and where you are headed, you can handle just about anything the world throws at you.

Ed's Life Challenge

One of my clients, Ed, is an entrepreneur who built a $100,000,000 distribution business. While building this business he made room for his wife, family, and friends. He loved to play golf and he played as often as possible. He attended church services regularly. He was financially secure and loved his business. He and his wife and children lived in a great community. Their home was everything he had ever imagined. The sacrifices he made in terms of time away to build his business were discussed and managed so that he and his family were in agreement. They found ways to stay connected and happy. It was all working until his wife was diagnosed with breast cancer.

The next few years were filled with worry and the ups and downs that a cancer diagnosis brings. Treatments were followed yet she succumbed to the disease. How did Ed survive? Ed had been completing an annual review of his life and had moved from a life that was hyper-focused on work and finance to improving his satisfaction in the other six life areas. The work he did on his life enabled him to find support to carry him through the grief. Family, friends, activities, church, his business, all were there for him. He did not depend on just one area, such as work, to fill his life. He knew that balance was key to his long-term satisfaction.

If you understand and work on each area of your life you will be able to move forward no matter what happens in the future. Even when you get a flat tire, you know how to fix it. Without balance you find yourself stuck, unproductive and unhappy.

Just as your mechanic discovers a belt that needs replacing before it fails and a doctor begins treatment for high blood pressure before it leads to a stroke, a comprehensive look at your life can uncover areas that, with a little attention, can improve your fulfillment and deepen your love of life.

MAPPING YOUR LIFE:
THE MISSION STATEMENT

Imagine getting on your bicycle and riding with no destination in mind. Yes, you will end up somewhere and you might even enjoy the ride and like where you end up. But that would be leaving your destiny to chance and luck. I had been doing just that for thirty-nine years and knew it was time to get a map out and decide where I was going with my life and how I would get there.

My work as a consultant and coach starts with asking my clients for a copy of their personal Mission Statement. My business clients know that they need a destination, a set of goals for their businesses. Yet, they were usually surprised when I asked for their personal mission statement. When they first bought their businesses they had a vision of what it would look like five or more years down the road. They put together a business plan and a mission statement to get there. Every business book and school shouts the importance of a "Mission Statement."

A mission statement lets you, your employees, your customers, your vendors, and your community know what is important. At the business level, my clients involve many people in the writing of the Company Mission Statement. This is done to gain buy-in for the mission. It works.

People want to know where the company is headed and how it will get there.

A very common interview question is, "Where do you see yourself in five years?" Of course, the question is about career and most interviewees can answer that question. A personal mission statement answers this question concerning where you want to be at the end of your life. The Boom Life methodology takes you on a journey every year to make sure you are on the path to completing your mission.

Your life needs a direction and a mission. Most people go through life without a written mission statement. Yet most people have a vision of what they want to accomplish with their lives. For example a vision of school, career, marriage, family, finances, and more are in your head. It is time to get it down on paper. Without a mission how will know you are taking the right steps to get there? You are the rider and, in this case, the writer. Let's look at two ways to tackle writing your mission statement.

The first way to write your mission statement is to take inventories of yourself and your life. Take some time and list the roles you have in life at this point. Here is my list: wife, mother, grandmother (my favorite role at the moment), business owner, consultant, coach, friend, aunt, sister, Catholic, community servant, traveler, student, teacher, speaker, and writer.

Write your list:

_____

_____

_____

_____

Now inventory the qualities and other aspects that you bring to these roles.

Here is my list: love, healing, friendship, trust, spiritualism, faith, intelligence, support, humor (at least I think I am funny), financial security, advice, knowledge, and respect.

Here is space to write your list:

_____

_____

_____

_____

Next list what you have accomplished or want to accomplish in your life.

Here is my list: raised my children, impacted my step-children, connected with family and friends, had fun with grandchildren, supported family and friends through hard times, travelled all over the world, ran a successful consulting business, assisted people in improving their lives, connected with my spiritual side, wrote a book or two or three and was a sought after speaker.

Here is space to write your accomplishments:

_____

_____

_____

_____

The next step is to combine these lists. Here is how I combined mine.

I am loved and I love my husband. We respect each other and truly enjoy being together. I am both a mother and grandmother who is loving and fun. My children and grandchildren love and trust me. My friends look to me for support and guidance as well as a good time. My business is successful and my clients prosper through my advice and knowledge. I have travelled all over the world, even to Antartica. I am a volunteer in the community. I take time to pray, meditate, and connect with my God and my church family. I love to read and learn and I am the author of several books that have been read by millions. I have spoken to groups of people from all over the world and touched their hearts and minds in a positive way.

Here is space to combine your lists and accomplishments.

_____

_____

_____

_____

_____

_____

_____

_____

The last step is to make this into a "Mission Statement." No matter how much you have achieved, continue to use your Mission Statement as the road map for your life.

My Mission Statement

> *To be a supportive and loving spouse. To enjoy my children who know how to be happy and successful in their lives. To impact my grandchildren and provide them with love and fun times. To provide my clients with the knowledge and skills they need to become more effective in their work and in their lives. To practice my religion through prayer and good works. To leave a legacy through books I have written, speeches I have made and through my family. To continue to learn, travel and enjoy my life with my husband, friends and family.*

Alternative Method for Writing Mission Statement

Another methodology to write your mission statement is to think about your eulogy. What do you want your family, friends, co-workers, customers, etc. to say about you and the life you led?

When I gave Bob, my husband, this assignment his first reaction was "That is morbid!" After he settled down and thought about it a bit, he got it. For Bob, competency in everything he is doing, did, and will do is key to his satisfaction with life. He began to write his eulogy, which looked like this.

Bob was a loving husband and father who provided for his family. If they needed anything, all they had to do was ask Bob. He provided financial support as well as (sometimes unsolicited) advice. Bob was a constant learner, always believing that he might know enough, but not everything there is to know. With this attitude, Bob absorbed as much information as possible through travel, people, reading, lectures, magazines, papers, TV, and news. His need to be competent in all subjects drove his love of learning. He was an avid gardener, sailor, and chef. He was a competent athlete, but not a star. He loved every New England sports team and was faithful to them even in the "dark times." His passion for competency also drove his business. Creating and developing a business that was grounded in solid business practices, staffed with people who were engaged in serving their customers, and providing consulting services that made client practices more effective and therefore more financially rewarding was a major focus of Bob's life. Bob's legacy is seen in the success of his customers, in the knowledge he has imparted to others, and just as important is reflected in his children, grandchildren, and great-grandchildren.

Taking the above eulogy, his mission statement morphed into this mission:

- To provide emotionally and financially for my wife and family;
- To enjoy life through gardening, sailing, cooking, and watching New England sports;
- To provide consulting services to improve the businesses of my clients;
- To create a business that is sustainable and adds value to staff;
- To continue to learn until the end of my life.

Write Your Eulogy

_____

_____

_____

_____

_____

As you can see there are many ways to tackle your own personal "mission statement." Take some time now and write your own. It may require a few tries and you may need to ask people close to you for their opinions, but that is more than O.K. As the author of _Seven Habits of Highly Effective People,_ Stephen Covey says, begin with the end in mind. Wise advice.

My Mission Statement

_____

_____

_____

_____

_____

_____

_____

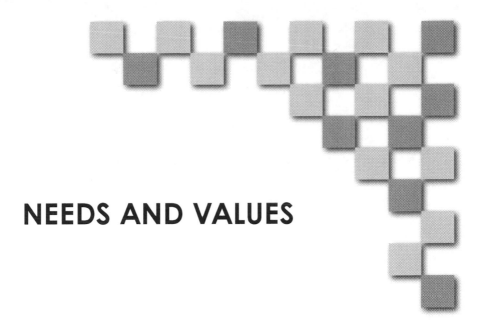

NEEDS AND VALUES

As you examine your life it is wise to get in touch with your needs and values. A need is an object, feeling, or circumstance that you require to achieve more satisfaction in your life. The Boom Life methodology is designed to help you assess your needs in eight life areas: Health, Living Environment, Career/Work, Finances, Social/Fun, Family, Intimacy, and Spirituality. A need is different than a want, in that you must have a need met, while a want is desired but not necessary for minimum life satisfaction.

Betty was a human resource executive at a large agricultural dealership. She suddenly found herself as a widow and a single parent. She realized that she would have to re-examine her financial needs and do it very quickly. She determined the minimum income she and her family required for them to continue their previous lifestyle. This was what she wanted. When she realized that she could not continue their previous lifestyle, she then broke down their basic needs: home, food, clothing, and the like. With this knowledge, she determined that to meet their needs on her current income the family would need to move to a smaller home. It wasn't what she wanted but it was what was needed. She realized that her financial needs were met for the short term but she had to plan for the long term: college for the kids, a wedding for her daughter, and retirement for herself. So she began to plan her financial future while keeping all other life elements in mind.

You can live without your wants but not without what you need. As you move through this program you will determine your needs. Your needs become your baseline for satisfaction. In Maslow's Hierarchy of Needs he states that you must satisfy each set of needs in sequential order. Here are the needs in their proper order:

First to be satisfied is Physiological then Safety and Security then Belongingness and Love then Esteem and finally Self-Actualization. Maslow also states that a satisfied need is not a motivator so in order to enhance your life use Boom Life.

Physiological needs include: food, shelter, good health, and other physical needs. Safety and Security needs include living without fear of harm and being confident that your physiological needs will continue to be met. Belongingness and Love involve family, intimacy, friends, and community. Esteem revolves around your need to feel a sense of accomplishment. Self-Actualization involves your need to pursue your Life Mission and realization that you are part of a greater power. Satisfaction in each of these areas starts with having your basic needs meet at the level below and then adding those extra "wants" to increase your satisfaction. When a level is satisfied it is not considered a motivator any longer. Using "Boom Life – A Guide to Life-Enhancement" will provide the motivation you need.

Remember my husband Bob's Mission Statement? He was in touch with a major need–the need to be competent, which is at the "esteem" level. He had satisfied his needs at the Physiological, Safety and Security, and Belongingness and Love levels, so his focus was more on Esteem. This need for competence can be found in all eight elements in his life. If you re-read your Mission Statement it will provide you with major clues to your needs and values.

Values are who you are. You use your values to live your life. So, it is very important that you realize what values are driving your behavior. Understanding your values will help you identify ways to create satisfaction. Living a life that is not connected to your values creates anxiety, confusion, and unhappiness. For example, one of my son Matthew's top values is honesty. His first job after college was in automobile sales. He was provided with a process to bring customers right up to the point of purchase and then turn them over to his manager. To do

> *"Your beliefs become your thoughts,*
> *Your thoughts become your words,*
> *Your words become your actions,*
> *Your actions become your habits,*
> *Your habits become your values,*
> *Your values become your destiny."*
> — *Mahatma Gandhi*

this, he had to tell half-truths about not knowing certain pricing, etc. He only lasted three weeks. He started to have headaches and his anxiety about going to work was growing and growing. When he realized how important it was to him to be 100 percent honest, he also realized that his current job was not for him.

What are your values? Below are thirty-seven values with space for you to add three more values if you want. Your first step is to pick your top twenty values and put an X next to each one.

Item	Value	X	Item	Value	X
1	Accuracy		22	Logic	
2	Achievement and Status		23	Loyalty	
3	Action and Adventure		24	Order and Organization	
4	Beauty and Art		25	Passion for Adventure	
5	Competence		26	Passion for People	
6	Cooperation		27	Peace and Quiet	
7	Creativity		28	Peace and Serenity	
8	Emotions and Feelings		29	Positive Attitude and Hope	
9	Excitement and Challenge		30	Power and Authority	
10	Facilitator, Teacher and Coach		31	Purpose and Meaning	

11	Fame and Notoriety		32	Responsibility and Accountability	
12	Flexibility		33	Self-control	
13	Forgiveness		34	Service to Others	
14	Freedom		35	Simplicity	
15	Generosity		36	Stability	
16	Growth and Change		37	Tolerance	
17	Honesty and Ethics		38	Truth and Honesty	
18	Humor		39	Wealth	
19	Influence and Impact on Others		40		
20	Justice and Fairness		41		
21	Knowledge and Learning		42		

Now go back to your top twenty and circle your top ten. Yes, it's challenging, but you have to eliminate ten values. This does not mean that you are letting those values "go." You are prioritizing your top ten values. If you are having a hard time, then ask yourself the following question, "If I had to live my life with either this value or that value which would I choose?"

Then go back again and check off your top five values. O.K., this may be getting very hard but you can do it. Now, circle the number of your top three values and finally put a big star on your number-one value.

Go back to your mission statement and make sure that your values are integrated within it. Can you see your number-one value in your mission statement? If so, that's great. If no, that's O.K. That's part of the process. Now that you are aware of the discrepancies, you can go back and write an even better mission statement for your enhanced life.

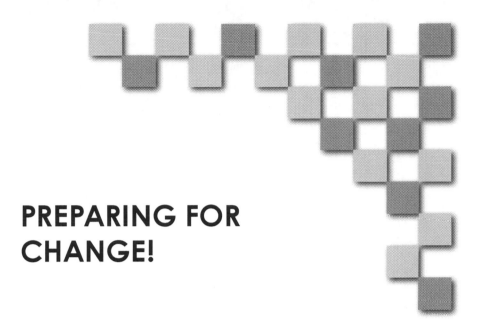

PREPARING FOR CHANGE!

This is the really cool stuff. I'm not going to use a lot of scientific jargon but if you are interested in the "science" you can look all this up. Science has now proven what I am about to reveal to you. Ready?

There is a physical part of our brains where we store our past learning and experiences as well as information that was there when we were born. Let's call this our operating system. This part of our brain, has as its major function, to keep us safe and alive. We use this part of our brain to get us through life and for the most part it functions really, really well. We are mostly not conscious of using our operating system.

Here is an example. Have you ever gotten in your car to drive home from work after having a hard day and as you pull into the driveway you have no recollection of driving on the highway? Have you ever lost your temper with someone and then wonder why you reacted so strongly? Have you ever felt tension in your shoulders when you pass by a dark alley alone? All of these events are controlled by your operating system.

Here is what happens: a person or situation triggers some sort of automatic thoughts. These thoughts then trigger a physical response, usually tension somewhere in the body. This tension then triggers a specific behavior. Here is an example.

Bill's Temper

One of my clients, Bill, complained that he was losing his temper at work. It was to the point that he would flare up with direct reports, peers, customers, and even his boss. He feared he would lose his job. This would happen so fast that Bill really felt out of control. We put together a plan to help Bill find out what was programmed in his brain that was getting him to react this way. I asked him to write down the following after he lost his temper: who was involved; what was said; how he felt physically; what thoughts came into his head; and how he behaved. He had to do this for two weeks. Then Bill would read over his journal and see if any patterns rose to the surface.

Bill called me at the end of two weeks and he was so excited. He figured it out. First, it didn't matter who was involved. What mattered was what was said or implied. Whenever anyone said or implied that Bill was lying he would tense up, clench his jaw, make fists, and get ready to fight. The thoughts that were triggered in his head (he only realized this by taking the time to think about it) sounded like this: "This guy thinks I am lying. Who does he think he is? Why does he think I am a bad person?" His response was to yell back, and get extremely aggressive and defensive.

As Bill thought about this, he remembered that growing up his mother (it's always the Mom's fault, ha!) had told him that lying was evil and that only the worst people were liars. This message had been programmed into his operating system. So when someone even implied that he was lying, he would get angry and defensive. These negative thoughts were based on a set of beliefs that his mother instilled in him when he young. The overriding belief was that liars were very bad people. When I asked him how this was working for him the answer was easy: it wasn't. This takes us to another part of our brain, the executive.

We use the executive part of our brain to think conscious thoughts. Bill now had to put his executive to work. He needed to update his operating system. He needed to stop his extreme reaction by becoming conscious of his body's tension, listening for the triggering message, and then replacing his automatic thoughts with a more appropriate thought, which would calm his physical tension and create an effective behavioral response. Here is how it went.

When Bill was confronted with a customer who implied that Bill had lied about the delivery date for his machine, Bill felt his hands tighten into fists and his jaws clench. Bill then told himself that the customer was just frustrated and that the customer did not really think Bill was an evil person. This allowed Bill to relax a little and he then could involve his executive to respond to the customer's frustration in a calm way and thus correct the problem.

As Bill did this more and more often he found that implying that he was lying was no longer triggering angry outbursts. He had successfully reprogrammed his operating system. Success.

As you move through this workbook you will be looking at your operating system (your set of core beliefs about yourself, life, people, and more) and taking some time to bring your programming (beliefs) into your consciousness. In other words, you may find that you need to upgrade your operating system to accomplish making life changes. Some of these changes will be scary; our operating system is designed to keep us safe, so when we are scared we usually run or fight. This "running" or "fighting" will only keep us tied to what may be causing dissatisfaction in our lives.

"If you want something new, you have to stop doing something old."
Peter F. Drucker

Throughout each section you will confront important questions to reveal behaviors that don't work for you anymore and behaviors that you may need to initiate. If what you have been doing is not effective anymore you need to change it. You will determine what belief you have that is driving that behavior, bring that belief into your consciousness, and then rewrite

19

it into a positive one. As you learn this method, your life will change for the better. There will be a sense of control and peace that you may not have experienced before learning this method. A healthy dose of daily self-reflection and positive thinking are just what we all need to improve our lives. Make it a habit and you'll live the life you want.

NAVIGATING
NEGATIVITY AND STRESS

Looking at the eight life areas in this book may bring out the Negative Nelly or Ned in you. This process is not meant to look at everything that is going wrong with your life, but rather to assist you in a realistic look at your life and in uncovering ways to enhance it. If you focus only on the negative, your stress levels will rise and so will your automatic thoughts about "I can't do this, it is too hard." As I said before, you will feel physical symptoms of negativity and it is called stress. Stress is often confused with tension. Tension is normal. We use it to keep ourselves sharp and moving forward. Think of an elastic band. Elastics need enough tension to do their job properly. Too little tension and the elastic does not hold. Too much tension and the elastic breaks. Just like an elastic band, we need to utilize tension in a positive way to complete our tasks. If there is no tension, we can become disinterested in our goals. If there is too much tension, it turns into stress.

A Quick Fix

Arthur, a limo driver, and I were discussing his job. When he rated his satisfaction with it he gave it a two out of five. I asked what the reasons for his rating were. Here are his first three responses:

1) He hated traffic.
2) He didn't like working for someone else.
3) He would rather be fixing cars than driving them.

As he stated these three negatives, I asked how he was feeling. The answer was: stressed. He said his hands got sweaty and he could feel tension in his upper back. His operating system was now rolling along with a list of negative characteristics of his job and his life.

I asked him to stop. I said, "You rated your job a two which means it isn't a one. What do you like about it?" A few seconds were required for him to change the direction of his thoughts but here are the top three things he likes about his job.

1) He likes his clients.
2) He likes the extra money because he can use it to play poker.
3) He likes the flexibility of the job.

I asked him how he was feeling now. He said that he could actually feel his body starting to relax. What was his takeaway? He now knew that negative thoughts brought on the stress and positive thoughts brought on a sense of peace. A huge lesson for Arthur. He even wanted to go back and change his rating to a four.

Stress is a part of life and so it is to your benefit to learn how to reduce stress and increase your sense of calm and peace. What do you do to relieve physical and mental stress? Yoga, run, bike, dance, laugh, read or play golf? It doesn't matter as long as you have a method of reducing physical stress.

One method that is highly effective and can be used by anyone anywhere is "belly breathing." To do it, just take in a breath through your nose while expanding your belly and then blow the breath out through your mouth while squeezing your belly in. Do this at least ten times.

It feels good, doesn't it?

Positive Thinking

Focusing on positive thoughts is crucial. To assist you with thinking more positively let's examine two concepts: positive affirmations and positive visualizations.

Affirmations and Visualizations

Affirmations are positive words about a subject or situation that we can repeat to ourselves over and over again. Repetition of an affirmation is one way to reprogram your operating (belief) system. Remember the children's book, *The Little Engine that Could*? Well that little train

"Olympians Use Imagery as Mental Training" By Christopher Clareyfeb

Visualization has long been a part of elite sports. Al Oerter, a four-time Olympic discus champion, and the tennis star Billie Jean King were among those using it in the 1960s.

But the practice of mentally simulating competition has become increasingly sophisticated, essential and elaborate, spilling over into realms like imagining the content of news conferences or the view from the bus window on the way to the downhill.

"The more an athlete can image the entire package, the better it's going to be," said Nicole Detling, a sports psychologist with the United States Olympic team.

You can find the entire article at http://www.nytimes.com/2014/02/23/sports/olympics/olympians-use-imagery-as-mental-training.html?_r=0

used a positive affirmation, "I can do it, I can do it," to move the train with its heavy load up the steep hill. What will you say to yourself when you begin to think of life changes that you want to make? Will you say, "I can't do that, it is too hard"? Or, will you say, "I can do that, it is within my power"?

Visualization is a critical element to the success of Olympians. When an Olympic athlete is training they are taught to visualize their performance. They close their eyes and not only "see" themselves running the perfect race, swimming their fastest, jumping their highest or skating perfectly, but they can smell it, feel it, and hear it. It has been proven that when they run through their physical performance in their minds, a connection to their muscles are triggered and muscle memory takes place.

Can you visualize playing with your children or leaving work at six and being "present" with your family for dinner? Can you visualize yourself working out three times a week and feeling your body getting stronger? Can you visualize reconnecting with family and friends that you have pushed aside? Can you visualize yourself successful, happy, and healthy? I hope so. If not, you will learn to do it here.

At the end of each chapter there will be the opportunity for you to write your own personal positive affirmation as well as your visualization. As you incorporate changes into your life, these affirmations and visualizations will become your new operating system.

Below are my gifts to you as you start this process.

Positive Affirmation - My life is my own and I make decisions to live a balanced, purposeful life.

Visualization - I see myself reading and re-reading this book and taking my time to really work the chapters. I hear myself asking others their thoughts on my life. I can feel the pen in my hand as I write my answers. I feel my satisfaction with life increasing. I am smiling more. It is easy to be calm and focused.

WORKING THE PROCESS

I would like to suggest two ways for you to get through this workbook with a high degree of efficiency and effectiveness.

The first way is to read through the workbook and complete each chapter. When you finish the entire book, go back and pick a chapter that you really want to work on - re-read it - review your action steps, beliefs - visualizations. Then spend the next month just focusing on that chapter. Here is an example.

Jack went through the workbook fairly quickly and when he was finished he decided to focus on the Spiritual Chapter because that had received his lowest score and he felt working on that chapter would improve other areas of his life. Jack's action steps were to attend church services weekly, pray or meditate daily, and to read books about spirituality.

Jack also thought that this was going to be the easiest chapter to focus on and improve. He began by going to church services and talking to other participants. He found that he missed the community feeling that participating in church activities had when he was growing up. He talked with his minister and asked for some reading suggestions. He found himself feeling calmer, more peaceful. His intent to pray or meditate every day became very easy. He spent several months just focusing on spirituality.

When he went back to the workbook to choose another chapter, he realized that just focusing on the Spiritual Chapter improved his Social/Fun, his Family, and his Intimacy life areas. A wonderful benefit. He really understood how all the life areas are linked and so he chose his next area and so on and so on. The process became part of his life. He uses the workbook now as a guide and a way to enhance his life on a continuous basis.

The second way to use this book is to complete a quick "off the cuff" assessment of each of the life areas. Use the chart below and rate each life area on a scale of one to five. Here is a chart to record your rating.

Life Area	Rating
Health	
Environment	
Career	
Finances	
Social/Fun	
Family	
Intimate Relationship	
Spirituality	

Then - go to the chapter where you scored the lowest and begin there. Complete that chapter and work on your action steps for a few months. When you feel you have improved your satisfaction in that life area, move on to the next one.

There is no one way to complete this workbook. Trust your gut and follow it. The only way that will not work for you is if you do not work the book. So, commit to enhancing your life and enjoy the ride.

HEALTH

Health Rating

Let's get started with the Chapter on Health. We are bombarded with messages that say we need to exercise more and eat better to look better and live longer. The cost of health care is outrageous and our ability to detect disease early and either control or cure it is (hopefully) the goal of our medical community. With all the data flooding us concerning how harmful smoking, sugar, fat and stress are, it is no wonder that many of us just shut down and stop listening altogether. The reality is that we need to pay attention to our health and hopefully before something knocks us down. To keep ahead of things, and have the strength and energy to move throughout the rest of this book, let's begin with our health.

The saying goes that if you don't have your health nothing else matters. I am not a believer of this philosophy. Here is why.

Conrad's Wild Ride

My Dad, Conrad, was diagnosed with non-Hodgkin's lymphoma when he was fifty. He went into a deep depression and started to distance himself from his family and friends. He lost his motivation at work. He was angry with God. One year and six months later, while he was getting his second cancerous tumor removed, my brother, his son, was killed in an automobile accident. My father stood beside my brother's casket and cried over the lost time he had spent feeling bad for himself instead of reaching out to his family and friends.

After my brother's death, my father reached out to those he loved every chance he had. He wrote up to ninety letters a month. He called his brothers every week like clockwork. He continued his passion, which was photography. The doctors told him he would have ten good years. Dad beat their prediction and lived another thirty years.

During those thirty years, Dad dealt with many setbacks in his health: four reoccurrences of the lymphoma, two heart attacks, quadruple by-pass surgery, prostate cancer, two bouts of bladder cancer, and the worst was kidney stones. Throughout all of that he learned never to stop living while he still had life left.

The doctors wanted to know my father's secret. Dad said it was simple. Keep your life in balance and have a vision of the future. Dad would focus on "making it" to an event a year or so in the future. For example, he would envision himself taking a trip or attending a wedding or the birth of a great grandchild. He could see himself there. He could feel the emotions that he knew he would feel. It gave him thirty more years of a wonderful life. My dad taught me that no one knows when their life will be over and in what order those you love will depart from this life, so live every day until you die. To do this, balance is so necessary.

There are other examples of living a balanced life even when your health is not great. Here is a partial list of shining examples: Steven Hawkins, Christopher Reeve, and Michael J. Fox. I know that Christopher Reeve lost his battle but look what he did while confined to a wheelchair: he was connected to his wife and family, he turned to prayer, he even acted, he became an advocate for spinal injuries and so much more. Michael J. Fox is another example of balancing his life with a chronic, debilitating disease.

Because of these inspirational people, I do not believe that if you don't have your health you have nothing. It is simply not true!

Brad's Weight Struggle

Brad complained about his weight all the time. He also had many excuses why his weight had ballooned to 250 pounds from 190 pounds in the last five years. Some of those excuses were: "I travel a lot and have to eat in restaurants all the time" "I am too tired to exercise." "My wife is a great cook and she loves to cook for me." These are just a few of them. As we began this chapter, Brad talked about all that he knew about healthy living. His knowledge was impressive about eating clean (no processed foods) and healthy exercise. He just wasn't doing it.

People who loved him tried to coerce him to lose weight by pleading and even insulting him, and that only made him mad. "They should just love me no matter how much I weigh."

Brad's doctor finally showed him that he was on the border of Type II diabetes, his blood pressure was high, and Brad's complaints about his knees were most likely a result of the added weight. Finally, Brad was ready to make some changes. But what changes? He began by rating his health using the questions below as his guide. He gave his health a rating of two.

Your Self-Assessment

Health is a broader subject than most of us realize. It encompasses more than whether we are sick or not. It includes our eating habits, physical condition, mental health, sleep patterns, stress levels, and our general appearance.

The following questions will help you think through your overall Health rating. You may find that one or two items are just great, such as your sleep patterns and exercise; but, your mental health may not be strong because of depression or anxiety, or you have a chronic illness such as diabetes, or some other physical disability.

Take all aspects of your health into consideration. When you are rating these areas make sure you factor in your satisfaction, which in health can be whether or not it is impeding your ability to live the life you want. So, you may have diabetes but if it is under control and doesn't stop you, then it might not impact your rating at all.

What follows is not an all-inclusive list. You may have items to consider that are not here. You know yourself best. You know how you feel. Sometimes it's only a matter of consciously checking in and asking, "How do I feel?"

- **Physical health** – Rate your physical health using the questions below as a guide.
  - o Do you see your doctor at least once a year?
  - o Do you adhere to taking any prescribed medications and/or vitamins?
  - o Do you have any chronic conditions such as diabetes, asthma, high blood pressure, or pain?
- **Sleep** – Experts all agree that we need sleep to function and be healthy. Consider your sleep patterns using the questions below as a guide.
  - o How many hours of sleep do you normally get? The biggest issue is having the same amount of hours every night.
  - o Do you go to bed and get up at the same time every day?
  - o Do you sleep through the night?
  - o Do you fall asleep easily?

The Centers for Disease Control and Prevention (CDC) and the National Institute of Health (NIH) have both conducted heart-related studies on people who have pets. The findings showed that pet owners exhibit decreased blood pressure, cholesterol and triglyceride levels -- all of which can ultimately minimize their risk for having a heart attack down the road. For those who have already experienced a heart attack, research also indicates that patients with a dog or a cat tend to have better recovery rates. These benefits are thought to be connected with pets' tendency to help reduce or at least control their owners' overall stress levels.

- **Diet** – We are what we eat!
    - o   Do you eat a healthy diet? How often? Most of the time with an occasional trip through the fast food lane or rarely because I am too busy.
    - o   Do you eat or not eat as a result of your stress levels?
    - o   Are you constantly on a diet?
- **Exercise** – We need to keep our bodies healthy by moving and using it.
    - o   Do you exercise on a regular basis? At least thirty minutes a day?
    - o   Is there exercise involved in your fun time? Playing baseball, swimming, dancing, walking, etc.
- **Mental health** – How we handle our emotions is important to our overall health.
    - o   Do you have a diagnosed mental illness? Are you taking the recommended steps to treat it such as medication or therapy?
    - o   How well do you handle the ups and downs of a typical day?
    - o   Do you feel balanced?
    - o   Do you consider the cup half full or half empty?
    - o   How do you handle life's crisis?
    - o   What do you do for healthy stress relief?
    - o   What causes you stress at work? At home?
    - o   Do you own a pet?

What is your rating using the following scale:

1 – Dissatisfied - The worst.
2 – Somewhat dissatisfied - Need to make big changes.
3 – Satisfied - I need to make some changes.
4 – Somewhat satisfied - Just a tweak or two will make things better.
5 – Satisfied - No action is needed right now because I am happy with where things are.

I rate my health a _____

Reasons for Health Rating

The next step is to write down the top three to five reasons that you gave this area of your life the rating that you did. This is not only for negative reasons but also for positive reasons. Then you will set a goal with every reason. For positive reasons it may simply be to continue the behavior. Then you will write down some actions steps that will assist you in achieving your goal associated with the reason.

For example, my dad, Conrad, rated his health a four for the following reasons:

Reason: I struggle with cancer from time to time as well as other health issues.
Goal: Survive.
Action Steps:
- Get check-ups.
- Listen and follow doctor's orders.
- Take all my medication.
- Stay in tune with my body and get help and answers when necessary.

Reason: I have a positive attitude.
Goal: Maintain my positive attitude.
Action Steps:
- Read one book every two months about positive psychology, such as "Buddha's Brain."
- Create boundaries for negative people that I must deal with.
- Hang around with positive people.
- Listen to motivational tapes once a month.

Brad was very enthusiastic and insightful when listing the reasons for his health rating of two. Here are a few of them.

Reason: I eat healthy food but I eat too much.

Goal: Reduce my portions.

Action Steps:
- When eating out, either eat half what I am served or order from the appetizer menu.
- Use a smaller plate at home.
- Increase my meals from three times a day to five times a day.
- No seconds.
- Learn to say "no".

Reason: I am not motivated to exercise.

Goal: Walk 3,000 steps a day and increase to 5,000 in three months.

Action Steps:
- Buy a "fit bit" or some other tool to track my steps.
- Buy a dog and commit to walking him/her twice a day.
- Find places for nice walks or hikes and ask friends and family to join me.

Use the table below to write down your reasons, goals, and the corresponding steps you can take to improve, continue, or stop behaviors that will lead to meeting the goal; include a time frame.

Reason #1_____

_____

Goal:	Time Frame
Action Steps:	

Reason #2_____

_____

Goal:	Time Frame
Action Steps:	

Reason #3_____

_____

Goal:	Time Frame
Action Steps:	

Reason #4_____

_____

Goal:	Time Frame
Action Steps:	

Reason #5_____

Goal:		Time Frame
Action Steps:		

Beliefs Regarding Health

Remember we move through life using our "operating system" that was programmed long ago with beliefs we may not realize drive our behavior. In this step you will look at each of your reasons and dig deeply to find the belief that is driving that behavior.

Conrad, my Dad, grew up in an era that believed cancer was a death sentence. Therefore, when he was first diagnosed with cancer, he was devastated. This belief sent the unconscious message that he was going to die and soon. This was why his first reaction was to enter a deep depression. It was his doctor who led him through the process of changing that belief.

As adults we need to acknowledge the original message and the behavior driving us, and then override it with a more appropriate message.

For example Conrad's new message is, "I am able to survive with the help of my doctors." Conrad had so many health events that it got to the point that he did not have to consciously think about surviving. His new message had become his belief system. This new belief then drove his behavior to listen and follow his doctor's orders.

This next step is tricky; take your time, and use a pencil so that you can go back and make changes as necessary. Here you will take each of the reasons you stated previously for your Health rating and you will write down what beliefs have been programmed into your operating system regarding that item. You will attempt to determine what it meant when it was implanted in your mind. After that, if necessary, rewrite the belief so it is more effective for you today.

As Brad examined his beliefs about food and portions, he was required to keep a log not only of how much food he was eating at a meal but the feelings and thoughts he had at the time. Brad began to realize that the portions he was served not only at home but at restaurants were much larger than most weight control programs required to lose or maintain a healthy weight. Yet, he would be compelled to eat everything on his plate. If he didn't eat everything on his plate he experienced anxiety. That anxiety made him moody. Of course in the process of working this chapter, Brad made a commitment to put less on his plate or to save and use leftovers when necessary. But there were times that this was not possible.

As he spent time reflecting on what was happening, he realized that when he was young his mother would tell him that people were starving in the world and that he should eat everything on his plate and not waste anything. This message told to him over and over led Brad to believe that to help the world and be a good person, it was necessary that he eat everything on his plate. When he left some food, he then felt as is he had failed to help starving people. When Brad realized this, he was able to use his executive function to rewrite that old belief.

His rewrite of his mother's old message was: "I am doing myself and the world the best when I eat an appropriate amount of food and reduce any waste." Now, instead of experiencing anxiety when he must leave food on his plate, he can look at the totality of his eating and see that he is reducing wasted food and that makes him a very good person. Brad worked hard at separating feelings of being bad with leaving food on his plate. It worked and now, he is losing weight without a lot of anxiety. As he sees it, this is a win/win for him and the world.

It is now your turn to reflect and write down beliefs that support or hinder your health goals.

Current Beliefs

Rewrite of Beliefs

Visualization

Here is where you get to have some real fun! Get into a comfortable position. Remove your shoes. Do not cross your arms or legs. You are the writer and director of your life. If you want more satisfaction with your health, see yourself healthy, feel yourself in good physical condition, taste healthy food choices, feel more energy, hear the doctor giving you great results from tests, feel a sense of happiness and peace.

Do you have a photo of you when you were healthy? Get it out and keep it visible. If you don't have one, then find a picture that is close to what your goal is, and post it in a visible place.

Example:

I see myself making good food choices when I go out to eat. This makes me feel proud of myself. I walk away from the junk food. I can see the numbers on the scale getting smaller. I see myself walking a half hour every day and I enjoy feeling more energy. I use my mind to keep a positive attitude that leads to feelings of happiness and peace.

What does your health visualization look like? Write down a few notes and have fun imagining the new you.

Positive Affirmations

I protect my health with good eating habits, exercise, and a positive mental attitude.

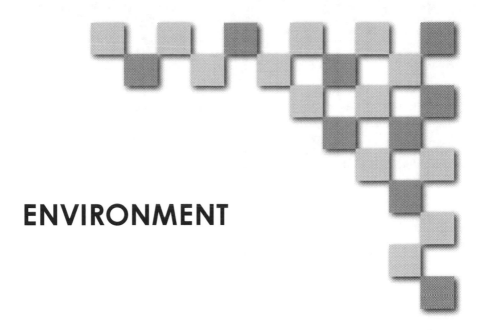

ENVIRONMENT

Environment Rating

What do I mean by environment? Well it is very broad. It takes into account where you are living in terms of country, state, city, as well as your home or apartment, and office. It is the ground floor of Maslow's Hierarchy of Needs. We all need a place to call home and those of us still working need a work environment that fits our motivational needs.

Environment is not only the physical elements that surround us, but also the culture that envelops us.

Where we are living has a significant impact on our lives. If you are a country person and find yourself living in an apartment in Manhattan you may find your mood and satisfaction are off balance. If you are in an area where you don't feel safe, this will have an impact on your life as well. You may have a partner that is messy, doesn't see the clothes piling up on the chair or the dishes in the sink, and this drives you crazy because you are neat and organized.

At work you may be internally conflicted if you work in a culture that does not match your values. Look back at the section where you identified your top values and use these values to determine if there is a good match between them and the values at work. For example, if your top value is "service to others" and your company believes in the motto that the customer comes first, you will feel a connection to the culture. It is a good fit.

Let's look at how environment has impacted two people.

Jennifer and the Forced Move

Jennifer is a young, soon to be single mom of two children, who moved out of her marital home into a rental home because of financial constraints. She owns her own business where she makes and sells her jewelry designs. She loathed her new home. She didn't want to move her children and she resented that her soon to be ex-husband would live in the house they had previously shared.

She did not feel good. Jennifer is normally a very neat person but she lost her desire to pick up and clean. After only a few months the rental home was beginning to show signs of neglect. Worse, she lost her motivation to make jewelry and her sales were falling. Jennifer was in a downward spiral and she didn't know what to do.

She and I talked for quite a while and it became clear to me that she had to make some changes in her environment in order to get back on track. After working with her and bringing the impact of her environment to her consciousness, she decided to make some changes. She invested some money in painting the first floor and replacing furniture (on a tight budget). What a difference it made. Within weeks of this change, her mood brightened, and her motivation was back. She created a new line of jewelry; she was back to cleaning and her sales went up significantly.

John and the Promotion

John was a different story. John was a parts manager at a branch of a large agricultural equipment dealership. He held that position for over thirty years. John was also a minority owner in the business and the business was growing rapidly. The executive team recognized that they needed to have a corporate parts manager to oversee the eight parts departments and to manage inventories. John was offered the position and he accepted the promotion to corporate parts management.

He was very excited but was finding it difficult to switch gears from managing parts at the store level to managing parts at the corporate level. For example, as a corporate parts manager he would be required to go on the road to visit with the other parts managers; but, with his office located in the same area as the day-to-day action he was "too busy" to get away. When I went to visit him at the dealership I saw that he hadn't moved his workspace away from the parts department. He was still taking calls from customers and assisting the counter parts staff in many ways.

I spoke to him about his need for an office space away from the parts department to allow him to focus on his new position; he was reluctant. He was so comfortable where he was that he feared a new environment would de-motivate him. It took several months but he finally moved from the parts area to an office on the second floor of the dealership. He left many items behind for the new parts manager. He put up photos in his new office of his family and scenes of the ocean he loved. He made sure that the office looked professional. He had the receptionist divert customers to the new parts manager and he limited his time spent down in the parts department. John now had the time to visit the other branch locations.

His new environment was exactly what he needed to remain focused on the corporate initiatives that would lead to dealership wide improvements. Without this change in environment, he would have continued to struggle.

Your Self-Assessment

How is your living environment and work environment affecting you? It is your turn to evaluate your environment.

Using the questions below, take some time to think about your living and working environment and then rate your satisfaction with it.

- **Living space** – The space where we spend our time has a tremendous impact on how we are feeling, - including the colors, style, and condition of your living space.

  > My favorite room in the house is the living room. We have two big couches, six recliners and more than 20 pillows. It's a really comfortable place to hang out with my family.
  > Cody Linley

  - o What is your clutter rating? How much clutter is around your house, room, etc.?
  - o Are you happy with your home/apartment/condo?
  - o How long is your "fix it" list?
  - o Do you feel safe at home?
- **Community (City/Town)** – This is the area surrounding your living space.
  - o Do you know your neighbors? Do you get along?
  - o Are you living in a part of the country that you prefer?
  - o Do you feel safe in your community?
- **Work Environment** – This is where you work.
  - o Do you feel comfortable and connected with the work culture?
  - o Does your workspace reflect who you are?
  - o Is your workspace organized? (A real time saver.)

What is your rating using the following scale:

1 – Dissatisfied - The worst.
2 – Somewhat dissatisfied - Need to make big changes.
3 – Satisfied - I need to make some changes.

4 – Somewhat satisfied – Just a tweak or two will make things better.

5 – Satisfied – No action is needed right now because I am happy with where things are.

I rate my environment a _____

Write down the top three to five reasons that you gave this area of your life the rating that you did. This is not only for negative reasons but also for positive reasons.

Reasons Regarding Environment Rating

Jennifer rated her environment a one-and-one-half. She cited the following: I live in a rental home but want to own my own home; I hate the color on the walls of the first floor; I don't like to go home because all the clutter makes me uncomfortable; my old furniture does not fit in this home; I love the décor of my store. Reasons had to be something she could control.

Under each reason she wrote down some steps she could take to improve, continue, or stop whatever the reason may be.

Reason: My home is cluttered.
Goal: To have a space I'm excited to go home to.
Action Steps:
- I will de-clutter for one hour each day until there is organization and room.
- I will not buy anything new unless I can throw something out.

Reason: The color of the first floor makes me nauseous.
Goal: To create a space that helps me feel peaceful yet energized.
Action Steps:
- I will set aside some money and buy a few gallons of paint.
- I will ask for help to paint the walls of the first floor.

John had rated his environment a four. Here are a couple of his reasons.

Reason: My family and I live in a great house that fits our needs and style.
Goal: Keep the house updated and in good working order.
Action Steps:
- Perform routine maintenance.
- Support my wife in updating rooms.

Reason: My office is right in the middle of the parts department and people see me as way too available.
Goal: Have an office where interruptions are reduced and I have time to do my new job.
Action Steps:
- Move to the second floor office -in the next month.
- Add elements to the office like my photos and certificates.
- Paint the office a color that I like.

It is now your turn. What are the reasons you rated your environment what you did?

Reason #1_____

_____

Goal:	Time Frame
Action Steps:	

Reason #2_____

_____

Goal:	Time Frame
Action Steps:	

Reason #3_____

_____

Goal:	Time Frame
Action Steps:	

Reason #4_____

_____

Goal:	Time Frame
Action Steps:	

Reason #5_____

Goal:		Time Frame
Action Steps:		

Beliefs Regarding Environment

Our beliefs will drive our programmed behavior. These beliefs come to us in the form of thoughts and feelings from which we react automatically. We will need to examine these beliefs to determine which ones are still effective and which ones we need to eliminate or change. Let's look at Jennifer's and John's beliefs.

Jennifer believed that if you rented a place to live you could not do anything to the space. She believed that it was up to the landlord to make any and all changes. This belief came from her friends who had rented apartments in the past. She was not aware of how this belief was driving her opposition to making changes in the house she was renting. After she discovered this, she changed her belief to, "It is okay to make changes to a rental property with permission." This change in belief freed Jessica to make the changes that improved her mood.

As John and I discussed his need to move his office away from the dealership parts department I asked him to reflect on the messages that came immediately into his mind. He noted that when he thought of moving his office, he heard "The parts' staff need me; they can't do this without me being near them." As this message became conscious he realized that he did not believe that the parts staff was competent. Wow, he was shocked. The belief that his staff was not competent had him behaving as a micro-manager. It was all wrong.

He re-wrote the message and thus the belief to the following: "My staff knows what to do and how to do it. I need to get out of their way so they can do their jobs." As John repeated this new message over and over, he became more confident in moving away from his previous office and job. It took a few months but he did it.

It is your turn to pull apart some of the beliefs that are driving your behavior - the good and the bad. This is the first step in changing the belief and therefore the behavior.

Write in the chart below the beliefs that you received about Environment. Rate each message as positive or negative or both. Take all the negative beliefs and re-write them or let them go.

Current Beliefs

Rewrite of Beliefs

For the next month, take note of when a behavior gets in the way of your goals and track it back to a belief you might have received. Remind yourself of the re-write of that belief and soon it will drive improved behavior and get you to your goals. Sometimes it is not possible to change your environment such as moving to a different location or buying a bigger house. What do you do then? You make the best of the situation and then work the steps to get you where you want to be.

Visualization

With this section, I suggest you create a detailed visual in your mind. You may want to acquire tangible cues to serve as a reminder of what you are working toward. For instance, if you are like me, your desk is a challenge. Clean it up and take a picture of it so that you have a visual of your ideal work environment. You can also find the pictures of your perfect environment and put them together. Then hang up your visuals where you will see them every day.

When my husband and I were first married we were living in a three bedroom raised ranch. It was about 1800 square feet of living space. Bob hated it! As soon as he moved in he started telling me about the home we would be moving to in a few years. It would be at least 3,200 square feet. He often described it in great detail. Both of us had just gotten divorces and our credit was not in a good place, so I didn't believe it was possible; but he did. He continued to paint this picture of a master bedroom with our own bathroom and so much more. It worked. In three years we were moving into a 3,400 square foot center hall colonial! Visualize your environment.

Positive Affirmation

I deserve to live and work in an environment that fits my dreams and my life.

CAREER/WORK

Career/Work Rating

If you are lucky enough to be retired, skip this section. If you are not happy with what you are doing for work, I suggest that you use this section to help you think through what you want to do or be, and, what you expect to get from a job/career.

If you have a career, this section is important to drive increased satisfaction. A wise man, my dad, once told me that there were only two reasons to work. One is that you love the work you do and the other is that the work you do provides you with the time, money, or whatever, to do what you love. This boils down to the issue that everyone needs a passion.

For some, that passion is their work. For others, their work provides them with the ability to do what they love. If you do not fall into either of these categories, your satisfaction with your career will be very low. Where do you fall?

It is important to realize that work is natural for people. It is part of our DNA. Whether you work for pay, as a volunteer, or for fun people seek out work.

James Facing the End of His Career

James is the owner of a very successful material handling dealership. He started as a salesperson back in 1975 and bought the single location dealership in 1982. James was just offered $50,000,000 for his business. He was facing the end of his career as the owner-operator of his organization. When we talked about the opportunity for him to take the money and retire, his response was very telling: "If I take the deal, I will just be an old guy with $50,000,000. If I stay and continue to work, I will be the owner and president of a large, successful company."

It was during this conversation that James realized that he lacked enough balance in his life to take advantage of this opportunity and feel good. He had focused so much time and effort on his career and business that he hadn't developed any outside interests. He was married for the second time and he and his wife were doing well but they had each spent too much time working and not enough time with friends, family, and in other areas of life. They would feel lost without work.

In this case, James rated his career very high. At the same time, other areas of his life were rated low. He needed to examine his beliefs and messages about work/career so that he could move to the next adventure in his life.

> Far and away the best prize that life has to offer is the chance to work hard at work worth doing.
> Theodore Roosevelt

We will look at this a little later in this chapter.

Patricia's Career Change

Patricia came to me while she was a front-end manager at a large department store. Her duties were to manage all the cashiers. She was not very happy. She did not find the work fulfilling, yet it gave her the money she needed to live and to ride her horses. Her rating of her career was in the mid-range of two-and-a-half to three.

Patricia is a single young woman with a college education and a passion for horses and the outdoors. As we talked, she expressed an interest in a career as a Ranger. It looked as if that would be a great fit. Patricia began to explore careers as a Ranger. The biggest drawback wasn't that she would have to move, but that starting wages were on the low side. She used the chapter on Finances to determine if she could make the career move and found it would be tight the first few years but doable.

She applied for positions at national and state parks. It took some time and lots of interviews but she was offered a job at Yellowstone Park and she took it. She tells me she is now living the dream because of going through this process. Her new rating for career is four. Her new focus is promotion.

Your Rating on Career/Work

Use the following categories and questions to assist you in your rating.

- **Appreciation**
  - o Do you feel appreciated at work?
  - o Are you paid a fair wage?
- **Satisfaction**
  - o Do you find the work you are doing satisfying?
  - o Are you doing what you were trained to do or went to school to do?
- **Work culture**
  - o Describe the atmosphere at work. Is it positive, negative, or neutral?
- **Work relationships**

- o   Do you get along with and respect your co-workers?
- o   What do you think of your co-workers – positives and negatives?
- o   Do you get along with and respect your bosses?
- o   What do you think of your bosses – positives and negatives?
- o   Have you formed friendships outside of work with any co-workers?
- o   What do you think of your customers?
- **Short and long term career goals**
  - o   Where are you in your career life? Beginning, middle, end?
  - o   What is the next step for you in terms of career?

What is your rating using the following scale:

1 – Dissatisfied - The worst.

2 – Somewhat dissatisfied - Need to make big changes.

3 – Satisfied - I need to make some changes.

4 – Somewhat satisfied - Just a tweak or two will make things better.

5 – Satisfied - No action is needed right now because I am happy with where things are.

I rate my career/work a _____

Reasons Regarding Career/Work Rating

Write down the top three to five reasons that you gave this area of your life the rating that you did. This is not only for negative reasons but also for positive reasons.

For example, James rated his career four! Here is a partial list of his reasons:

Reason: His career has provided him with the ability to take care of himself and many employees financially.

Goal: Create a business that can continue to provide financial security to employees without his ownership.

Action Steps:
- Hire and retain high performing executives.
- Continuous training of the management group.
- When transferring ownership make sure new owners have the same value system as he has.

Reason: He loves going to work.
Goal: To reduce his time at work to three days a week.
Action Steps:
- Develop a strong outside interest: golf, sailing, non-profit work. In other words, work the rest of this book and get some balance!
- Take many vacations. Some long. Some short.

After doing the evaluation, James, our powerful president of a thriving company, is now convinced that he can retire. He realizes it is never too late to achieve balance and he believes he can live the rest of his life in peace and have a sense of satisfaction and fulfillment. He knows that to do this he needs to work on other areas of his life. His balance was off and he needs to improve the other areas of his life to round out his tires and ride his bike with ease.

Here is how James rated the other life areas: Health = three-and-a-half, Environment = five, Career = four-and-a-half, Family = two, Social/Friends = four, Finances = four, Spiritual = two, Intimate Relationship = five. He is committed to improving his satisfaction with Family, Social/Friends and Spiritual: three life areas truly needed for full life satisfaction.

Patricia rated this section a two-and-a-half at the beginning of her Boom Life experience. Here are two of her reasons.

Reason: I don't like working inside all the time.
Goal: Work outdoors.
Action Steps:
- Assess and update my resume to highlight my education and passion.
- Research agencies that hire park rangers.
- Apply, apply, and apply.

- Don't give up.

Reason: I am good at what I am doing but it is not what I want to do.
Goal: Work in my field of study.
Action Steps:
- Research other careers that fit my degree.

It is now your turn to write your reasons for your Career Satisfaction rating, write down your goal for each reason, and then the action steps needed to get there.

Reason #1_____

_____

Goal:	Time Frame
Action Steps:	

Reason #2_____

_____

Goal:	Time Frame
Action Steps:	

Reason #3_____

_____

Goal:	Time Frame
Action Steps:	

Reason #4_____

_____

Goal:	Time Frame
Action Steps:	

Reason #5_____

_____

Goal:	Time Frame
Action Steps:	

Beliefs Regarding Career/Work

We will continue to believe what we were told as children about careers and adult behavior, unless we take steps to update these limiting beliefs. There are several beliefs about career/work that drive many of our behaviors.

Many of these beliefs are gender related or have been gender related. For men, "It is your responsibility to care for the family financially." For women, "Career comes second to taking care of the family." So if a man chooses to be a stay-at-home dad, his father may see him as a failure. If a woman chooses not to have children, but to instead focus her life on a career, her mother may see her as a failure. These are just two of the outdated beliefs our society still clings to regarding career.

Let's look at the beliefs that were driving James' behavior.

James grew up with a father who was what we would call a "workaholic." Any time that James complained that his father wasn't there for him (attending sports games, school programs, and such) James' father would say that it was his duty to provide for his family. James' dad made it clear that one day it would be James' duty to provide for his family and that he would have to make sacrifices to do that. This belief morphed into James' belief that providing for his family, without also sacrificing time with them was wrong. He felt that he was failing if he left work early or used all his vacation time.

When James became conscious of this message he was able to rewrite it. His new message is: My career provides for my family and when sacrifice is necessary (as it was in the beginning of his business) it does not measure my success.

As he let the old message go, he was more and more comfortable with focusing on the other life areas without guilt.

Patricia found that one of her beliefs was from messages she got from family and friends about her choice of a major in college. That belief was "You won't find a job in your field that will pay you enough to live on! Good luck!" This belief led her to abandon too quickly her quest to find a job as a ranger. She changed that belief to: "There is job in my field of study that will provide me a living wage." This new belief was instrumental in Patricia being confident that it was possible to find her dream job and she, therefore, could be committed to and patient in the search.

Let's pull apart some of the beliefs that are driving your behavior - the good and the bad. This is the first step in changing the message and, therefore, the behavior.

Write in the chart below the beliefs that you have about Career and the "hidden" messages that drive those beliefs. Take some time to think about it. Reflect on your last job and look into the process to find any beliefs you might have. For instance, old messages of "you can't do that" will translate into a belief that you aren't able to move ahead in your career. Get it?

Remember to take all the beliefs that are getting in the way of increased satisfaction and re-write them or let them go.
Current Beliefs
Rewrite of Beliefs

<table>
<tr><td></td></tr>
<tr><td></td></tr>
<tr><td></td></tr>
<tr><td></td></tr>
</table>

For the next month, take note of occasions that a behavior gets in the way of your goals and track it back to a message you might have received. Remind yourself of the re-write of that message and soon the new message will drive improved behavior and get you to your goals.

Visualization

Take some time to create the picture of your perfect career. What are you doing? Who do you work with? See yourself performing your job perfectly? It doesn't matter if you are working at your dream career right now - visualize what you want. When you are working on this chapter sit quietly once or twice a day and go through your visualization.

Positive Affirmation

I am capable of having the career I want. I have the ability and determination to take the steps necessary to get there.

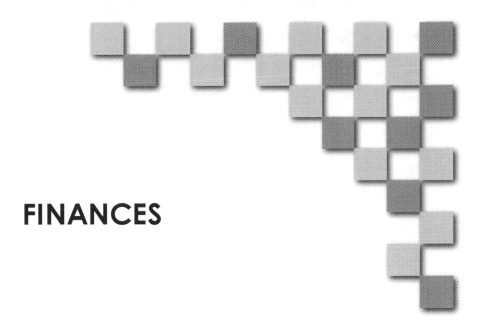

FINANCES

Finance Rating

It isn't how much money you make that is important; it is how much money you spend. This section is one of the most objective sections in the book. You will need to analyze whether you have enough money to provide for your basic needs, and, then determine what you need in the future, and what you want in your life that will have a monetary cost. Then work to get there.

There is a lot of help "out there" for you to use. If budgeting is not your thing, google it and find a budgeting tool that fits your needs. I use Quicken and others use Mint. If this chapter is mind boggling for you consider getting a financial planner involved. Don't be intimidated by financial institutions. They want you to be fiscally solvent, so ask for their help. Be proactive and reap the rewards.

This is also the chapter where, if you find yourself in trouble - such as losing your job and having to make severe cuts in your financial situation - your work in the other areas of your life will come in handy. Look to family and friends for advice and help (short term).

Joan and the Decision to Stay at Home with Kids

Joan has an advanced degree in counseling psychology. She has worked in research for many years at a local hospital and medical school. Joan is married and lives in a two-bedroom condo with her husband and three children. Before Joan became pregnant with their third child, her husband made the bold decision to buy a sports equipment store that was associated with two local hockey rinks. Joan provided health insurance, had a 401k, and supported the household while he grew his business. At the time, she rated their finances a three.

When Joan realized that she was pregnant for the third time, she went to this chapter and reviewed their financial needs. She really wanted to become a stay-at-home mom. Their review started with the budget they had put together concerning their necessary monthly expenses: mortgage, food, childcare, cars, insurances, utilities, phones, and the like.

She and her husband then recalculated their budget based on removing child-care costs and a reduction in expenses associated with one of their cars. Then they looked at what income would be generated from his business. It didn't look good. The deficit was significant in that first year. What did they do next? They looked at what they had in assets and liabilities and determined that there were assets they could liquidate short term to carry them through the first year and a half until his business was producing an adequate amount of income.

Decisions they made: use Joan's pension to supplement their income; put their condo up for sale and rent an apartment to free up any equity, get on an affordable health plan, focus on improving sales at the stores, and Joan would provide childcare part time to supplement their income.

Not everyone will agree with Joan's tactics but she is very happy she is home with her kids, and, has time to plan for a career change. She is managing the household finances very tightly and enjoying that process. She and her husband are more future oriented and are making decisions that are good for the short term and will drive long-term success.

Andrew and Living the Dream

Andrew was truly living the dream. His career was providing his family of four with a six-figure income. They lived in a desirable neighborhood, drove new cars, had a savings account, set aside money for retirement, and even more. Life was great on the financial front. Or, so he thought.

Our work together took us to this chapter and Andrew had a very high rating, a five. He wanted to skip over the work in this section and I wouldn't let him. He needed to make a deep dive into his financial picture and to truly understand and control his finances.

When he listed his assets and liabilities he realized the following: he was paying a higher interest rate on his mortgage than was currently available; he had credit card debt at interest rates over twenty percent; he wasn't maximizing his contribution to his 401k; and there were additional similar issues. It was a real eye-opener for Andrew. He realized that he needed to make some changes to maximize the benefits from his great income.

Andrew decided to refinance his home. He was able to reduce his monthly payments. He focused on eliminating his credit card debt and negotiated lower interest rates on the cards he would keep active. Lastly, he maximized his 401k contributions.

Andrew also began working with a financial consultant to prepare for his future. He learned that having a lot of money could lead to being lazy in managing it.

My Story

My story is a little different from Andrew's but on the same lines. When Bob and I decided to sell my raised ranch house, I went to a loan officer who is also my friend. I wanted to buy a new house on my credit only which would be challenging. She helped me understand how to read a credit report, how to clean it up, how long it would take, and what I had to do.

It took a year to get my finances in order and it was a soul-baring process. Why? Because I had to take a good hard look at where I was spending my money, how good I was at paying bills on time, and how much I owed on credit. At times I embarrassed myself with my lack of self-discipline. My ability to turn a blind eye to my poor financial behavior allowed me to continue spending without thinking and to ignore the consequences of late payments and high credit card debt. Taking the blinders off and becoming self-aware changed my behavior. I put a budget in place and followed it. I had reminders on when to pay bills so there were no more late payments. I focused on reducing my debt and increasing my personal equity. Now, I was ready to house hunt.

The next step was to determine how much I could get for a mortgage, what kind of budget I could afford in terms of utilities, taxes, insurances, etc.

I found two houses that fit my environment needs and my finances. I was in love with one of these homes but the seller would not take my offer because it was contingent on both the sale of my current home and final approval of a mortgage. I was very disappointed, but the second home would also fit my needs; that transaction went through without a hitch. I am thankful that I didn't get my first choice. The home we live in is a center hall Colonial with a great floor plan that works extremely well with our expanding family – five kids and their spouses, fourteen grandchildren, one great-grandchild, one dog; and at times a few house guests. The street we live on is a private street and in the desired section of the city. Not everyone lives with us - thank you, God. But we have had many people, including some with children, live on the third floor over the past fifteen years.

The story doesn't end there. I had been living in the home for about five years when interest rates started to drop significantly. My loan officer called me and said that it was time to refinance. When we looked at all the options, I decided to refinance my thirty-year mortgage into a fifteen-year mortgage and with the lower interest rate. My monthly payment actually went down slightly. I was able to pay a little more on the loan every month and further reduced the time to the payoff date.

Paying attention to my finances really paid off. Of course, my friend said that she wanted me to own my home free of financing before I was sixty so that I could think about retiring. My home is now paid off about eleven years earlier than my original mortgage. Certainly a win/win situation.

Your Rating of Finances

You can't spend more than you make or problems develop. You will need to do some research, data collection, and basic math in this section. So, grab your calculator and let's get to work.

- **Assets**
  - o You need to know what your worth is and that involves knowing what you own in terms of cash, home value, cash value of insurance policies, stocks, retirement plans, automobiles, boats, and personal items with a clear value.
- **Liabilities**
  - o How much do you owe and to whom? Make the list and note the interest rate being charged on all charge cards and loans: home mortgage, car loans, and the like
- **Savings**
  - o Do you have a savings account?
  - o Do you have enough saved to cover your expenses for a three month period?
- **Spending patterns**
  - o Do you carry cash? This is a great way to lose track of what you are spending your money on and how much.
  - o Do you buy things you want? Or just what you need?
- **Budget**
  - o How much money comes in every month?
  - o What are your monthly expenses? – Rent/mortgage, groceries, fuel, electricity, car payment, cable, internet, phones, child support, alimony, insurance payments, loans, credit card payments, mad money, and the like.
  - o What are expenses that get paid yearly or quarterly? For example, insurances, taxes, vacation, and holiday gifts.

- **Retirement**
  - o What are you doing to save for retirement?
  - o IRA, 401k, savings, life insurance, home equity, inheritance, etc.
- **Insurance**
  - o Is your family or estate protected with adequate insurance?
  - o Are your assets protected with adequate insurance? Home, car, liability?

What is your rating using the following scale:

1 – Dissatisfied -The worst.
2 – Somewhat dissatisfied – Need to make big changes.
3 – Satisfied - I need to make some changes.
4 – Somewhat satisfied - Just a tweak or two will make things better.
5 – Satisfied - No action is needed right now because I am happy with where things are.

I rate my finances a _____

Reasons Regarding Finance Rating

The challenge with finances is that they may be tied to your satisfaction with your career, which Joan rated very low at three. She rated her finances a four for the following reasons:

Reason: I pay my monthly bills on time.
Goal: Continue to pay debt on time.
Action Steps:
- Create a budget with due dates.
- Use online payment options to reduce chances of late payments.

Reason: I do not have a savings account.
Goal: Save three months' worth of expenses.
Action Steps:
- Open a savings account.

- Do not have access to it through debit card.
- Save $25 a week - no excuses.

Andrew's reasons for rating his finances a five were obvious to him. Things were going very well. He just needed to keep an eye on things.

Reason: I make enough money to cover our needs and our wants.
Goal: Continue my financial stability.
Action Steps:
- Focus on the Career section of this workbook to maintain my income
- Examine how my investments are performing on a monthly basis.

Reason: My credit score is great.
Goal: Maintain a great credit score.
Action Steps:
- Pay bills on time.
- Watch credit card spending.
- Negotiate better interest rates on all debt.

It is time for you to write the reasons, goals and action steps for your rating of your finances. As you can see from the examples given above, you rated your finances what you did for a reason. Now, you will need to determine what your goal is regarding that reason - do you want to continue the reason or change it? Write down your goal. To achieve that goal you will have to take some action. Determine a few steps that you need to take to achieve your goal.

Reason #1_____

_____

Goal:	Time Frame
Action Steps:	

Reason #2_____

_____

Goal:	Time Frame
Action Steps:	

Reason #3_____

_____

Goal:	Time Frame
Action Steps:	

Reason #4_____

_____

Goal:	Time Frame
Action Steps:	

Reason #5_____

Goal:	Time Frame
Action Steps:	

Beliefs Regarding Money/Finances

Some of the ways that we come to our adult beliefs about finances are from the messages that we learned as we watched our parents and how they treated money/finances. Other messages were very overt from our parents.

James grew up in a household that did not discuss finances. He remembers thinking that if you need money you drive to the bank, use a card, and get some. This perception led him

> *"I love money. I love everything about it. I bought some pretty good stuff. Got me a $300 pair of socks. Got a fur sink. An electric dog polisher. A gasoline powered turtleneck sweater. And, of course, I bought some dumb stuff, too."* –Steve Martin

to believe money is always there and available. This belief led to laziness. He rewrote this belief to be: "Money does not come with instructions or controls. I am in charge of what happens to my money."

Joan grew up in a large family where money was always a topic of conversation in terms of what they could afford or not afford at the moment. She believed that money needed to be managed and that it was in short supply. This perception has led to her enjoying managing her money. Joan did not change her message because it is serving her well right now; yet she does not want the belief that money is in short supply to stop her from making more money in the future. So she removed that piece from her message. It now reads: "Money needs to be managed and we have enough."

What were you told during your early years? Did you have an allowance? Did you have to save to get things you wanted or did you just have to bargain with your parents to get what you wanted? What beliefs did those behaviors create in you?

Let's pull apart some of the messages that are driving your behavior - the good and the bad. This is the first step in changing the message and, therefore, the behavior.

Write in the chart below the beliefs that led to your behaviors about Money/Finances. Rate each belief as positive or negative or both.

Take all the negative beliefs and rewrite them or let them go.

Current Beliefs
Rewrite of Beliefs

If you are in the process of getting your finances in order like I had to do, you will need to look at your finances monthly and note any changes to what you had planned. Once you have your finances under control you can take a "deep dive" quarterly, and then a solid review yearly.

It is also never too early to find a good financial planner!

Visualization

Picture your bank statement and investments with healthy balances, have a specific number in mind such as $1,000,000. Picture yourself debt free. Imagine how it will feel to retire without financial worries. See yourself getting that boat or vacation home.

Positive Affirmation

I have all the money I need and manage it effectively.

SOCIAL/FUN

Social/Fun Rating

If you happen to be a hermit skip this section. If you are still reading, I will assume that you are a social being and that your social life is important and/or that you like or would like to have more fun in your life.

Why is this life area important? Unstructured play is critical in healthy social development. Play is also the way children learn problem solving. As we grow and mature we tend to reduce our playtime because we might not think that we need it. But, we do need to play and to interact with other people. Play reduces stress, improves relationships and increases creativity.

What is Play?

At dinner one evening with several business clients I asked the question to three business owners, "What do you do for fun?" Their answers were interesting. Rich said that he played golf. He also said that it was fun for him to mentor other men. Kevin brought out his phone and showed me pictures of the Lego land that he had put together. Believe me when I say that it is very impressive. Jim said that his fun consisted of hunting and fishing as well as golf. I was happy that each man had a list of activities they did that they considered fun. I then asked how often they laughed and hung out with friends. This took more thought and they all responded the same. "Not often enough."

Friends are an indicator of a healthy life. Throughout my life, my friends have been such an important part of balancing on my life bike. They have been there to keep me sane during crises. They have held my hand and cried with me during losses. They supported me during times of change. They have challenged me to be better and do more and to have fun.

My Story

One of my closest friends, Annie, has been by my side for more than forty years. We met as young adults and bonded after the births of our firstborns. My life would have been so much harder without her in it. We supported each other through children, marriages, deaths, and work.

In fact, after the births of our second children (she laughed at me when I told her I was pregnant again and she found herself pregnant two months later - she didn't laugh when I got pregnant with my third) we were both unhappy in our marriages. My mother believed that Annie was influential in my decision to get a divorce because Annie had decided to leave her husband. Was it so? I don't think so.

Either way, Annie and I decided to move in together to support each other financially and emotionally. So, we lived on the third floor of a three-decker house with four children: two three-year-olds and two one-year-olds. It worked. We both had sitters for our children while we worked. We would alternate going out and babysitting for each other.

One time I actually made two dates for the same night - oops! I decided I wanted to go with one guy more than the other but I didn't tell the other guy. I left Annie at the apartment with the four kids and when my second date arrived she had to tell him that I was already out. Oh, I had told her that I had a surprise coming that night just for her. When he arrived, she shook her head and introduced herself to him and they spent the evening talking. They actually dated for a while.

We talked, laughed, cried, and at times only had peanut butter or pasta for food, but the rent was paid and the electricity was on (okay it got turned off maybe once or twice). We shared living quarters for about a year and a half but we continue to share our lives.

I have other friends that are also in this category. Not hundreds, just a few, but that is all I need. Friends have your back. Friends are there in good times and bad. Friends tell you the truth when you need to hear it and will lie when you need to hear a lie. Stop for a moment and think of your friendships. Who would drop everything and run to your side to support you in bad times? Makes you feel grateful, doesn't it?

Another aspect of this section is your involvement with your community. Now, that community may be your neighbors, local politics, a non-profit or a social club. Involvement with your community provides connection to a group larger than your family and even your social circle. As your needs are met for physical, security, and love you will find yourself looking for more and that more is giving back to others. I was asked to be on the Board of Directors of a start-up non-profit that helped families with small children who needed respite or care while the parent or guardian was unavailable. We used the model of an emergency nursery. I was able to put time, talent, and some of my money into this worthwhile venture. After two years of planning, organizing, and gathering contracts and funding, we opened. It was one of the most fulfilling experiences I have ever had. I got nothing out of it but this sense of helping others in need.

Here is one of the cases: a grandmother showed up in the emergency room very sick and needed to be hospitalized. She had with her a two-year-old grandchild who was in her custody. She was refusing to be admitted because a social worker would be called to take her grandchild into their care. There was no one else to help this woman. As a woman in her seventies she was terrified that she would not regain custody of her grandchild. The emergency nurse called us. We were able to go to the hospital, get permission to care for the child while the grandmother received treatment. The grandmother was able to talk to the child every day. The child was well cared for and returned to the grandmother in five days: such a successful event. What are you doing to give back?

Community, friends, fun, and laughter are necessary for your physical and mental health. Let's look at two examples.

Steve's Retirement

Steve retired from a utility company after thirty-five years of dedicated service. He was financially set due to long-term planning. He didn't expect to feel strongly about the loss of his career. The first few months of his retirement he filled his time with golf, his grandchildren, reading, and working around the house. But none of these activities provided Steve with the feeling of accomplishment that he felt at work.

Steve was also involved with the American Red Cross. He was on their board of directors and had volunteered his time over the years for various positions and events. There were changes happening at the chapter where he volunteered, so Steve's wife suggested that he get out of the house and ask the executive director if there was something that Steve could do to help.

The director was thrilled and immediately asked Steve to work on financial reporting. Steve was given an office and began putting in thirty hours a week. He is very happy. The feeling of accomplishment came back. The great thing is that it's not the same as a job. If he has other family obligations, he's free to do what he wants.

When Steve ended his career he realized that one of his values was accomplishment. As a result he turned to his Social/Fun Life Section and found that he needed to give back in order to feel complete and balance his life bike. Now he is working on developing the ways he feels a sense of accomplishment through more travel and more fun.

Teresa's Move

Teresa's husband came home and announced that he was given a great promotion and raise but that it would involve moving the family to another state. Teresa was excited for her husband and the raise, which would improve their financial position. Her next question was, "Where are we moving?"

Teresa and her family were living in a suburb of Dallas where they had many friends and family. They were involved in many community activities. The move was going to take them to a rural locale in Mississippi. The company paid for Teresa and her husband to spend a week in the new community to look for a home and become acquainted with the area and the people.

The second night, Teresa became more and more unsure of the move. The thought of leaving her friends behind caused her intense anxiety. She knew her family would always be there for her but she worried the miles would create a separation of more than miles between herself and her close friends. Also she was concerned about fitting in and making new friends. At forty-two, it can be more difficult to cultivate the type of friendships that grow from years and years of shared experiences.

She talked to her husband about her concerns and together they agreed that they would put a plan together that would keep their Dallas friends and family close (not in miles but in other ways) and they would use this plan to help their children adjust. They used the process in this book to discover that they had always believed that to be a close friend you had to be close geographically, and that you had to have consistent contact. They began to change their thinking about friendships and when they asked others and looked around they realized that friendships are not determined by distance or even time together. Friendships are determined by love, acceptance and understanding.

The plan was simple. They would make the trip back to Dallas at least twice a year. They would make sure their home had enough space to accommodate many guests. They would develop a call list and make sure to stick to it. They would post updates on social media and encourage others to share their lives as well. It would work!

On the third day in Mississippi, they went to a realtor to begin looking for houses. As they began to drive around the neighborhoods inspecting homes, the realtor asked about the children and what they were "into." Sports were covered. Dance was no problem. But one daughter was a cheerleader with the high school and she loved it. The realtor admitted that this was a potential problem. The local high school had lost their experienced cheer coach and was using the gym teacher. The kids were not advancing and were getting quite bored. Teresa then shared that she was a cheerleader in college and had been captain of the team and had done some coaching. It was a match!

Getting involved right away, and actively setting a plan to stay engaged in what was most important to them, paid off. Adjusting their thinking and beliefs about friendships worked to make them feel more positive about their move. The move went quite well because they were pro-active instead of reactive.

Your Rating Regarding Social/Fun

Use the list of questions to help you rate this life area.

- **Community**
    - o Do you have a "cause" that you help with or volunteer for?
    - o Do you belong to a social group such as Rotary, Masons, Lion's Club, Mother's Club?
    - o Are you on any committees?

- **Friends**
  - o How many friends do you have, other than family?
  - o How often do you see/talk with your friends? Is it often enough for you?
  - o Name the friends that you trust.
  - o Do your friends support you or criticize you every chance they get?
- **Fun**
  - o How do you have fun? Movies, sports, parties, learning, concerts, travel...?
  - o Who do you have fun with?
  - o Is there enough fun in your life?
- **Hobbies**
  - o Do you have a hobby such as painting, crafts, collecting, and others?
- **Activities**
  - o Are you involved in any activities? Sailing, dancing, fantasy sports, tennis, running, etc.
- **Downtime**
  - o How do you relax? Read, listen to music, or watch some TV...?

What is your rating using the following scale:

1 – Dissatisfied - The worst.
2 – Somewhat dissatisfied – Need to make big changes.
3 – Satisfied - I need to make some changes.
4 – Somewhat satisfied – Just a tweak or two will make things better.
5 – Satisfied – No action is needed right now because I am happy with where things are.

I rate my social/fun a _____

Reasons Regarding Social/Fun Rating

Steve had originally rated this chapter on social/fun as a two-and-a-half. Below are two of the reasons he rated it so and the goals that he established with some of the action steps he needed to accomplish to improve this life area.

Reason: I don't spend much time with friends.
Goal: Renew or develop relationships with Fred (and wife) and Sam.
Action Steps:
- Call both men every other week just to chat and catch up.
- Arrange golf with them monthly or sign-up for a golf league.
- Ask my wife for help arranging couple time.

Reason: I don't have much fun anymore.
Goal: Figure out what is fun for me at this point in my life.
Action Steps:
- Do something just for fun once a week.
  - o Movie, concert, lecture, sporting event.
- Try something new.
  - o Hiking, drawing, tennis.

Teresa on the other hand had very different reasons for her ranking of social/fun. Before the thought of moving she ranked this area a four-and-a-half: very high because she had close friends she could count on and have fun with. With the move about to take place her rating dropped to a three and here are her reasons, goals, and action steps.

Reason: I have lots of hobbies and activities that I can continue after my move such as reading, gardening, sewing, and running.
Goal: Continue with my activities and find others with the same interests.
Action Steps:
- Research gardening clubs.
- Find a running trail.
- Volunteer at the library and/or find a book club.

Reason: I will miss my Dallas friends and worry that we will lose touch.
Goal: Maintain my Dallas friendships.
Action Steps:
- Use social media to keep in touch on one level.
- Call friends on a weekly basis.

   -    Plan visits back and forth at least twice a year.

Write down the top three to five reasons that you gave this area of your life the rating that you did. This is not only for negative reasons but also for positive reasons. For example, if you rated your social/fun a four you might site the following: I have great friends. I play golf every week. Reasons have to be something that you can control. Then under each "reason" write down some steps you can take to improve, continue, or stop whatever the reason may be. Using our example from above, "I have great friends," you might write the following; "I will contact my friends weekly to keep in touch."

Reason #1_____

_____

Goal:	Time Frame
Action Steps:	

Reason #2_____

_____

Goal:	Time Frame
Action Steps:	

Reason #3_____

_____

Goal:	Time Frame
Action Steps:	

Reason #4_____

_____

Goal:	Time Frame
Action Steps:	

Reason #5_____

_____

Goal:	Time Frame
Action Steps:	

Beliefs Regarding Social/Fun

What do you believe about friendships, having fun and community involvement? These beliefs are rooted in your past and the messages we saw and heard. These beliefs will drive how we behave, and so, we need to examine them to effectively change our behavior.

Sometimes we take the actual words of the message and put an implied meaning to it that may or may not be what the sender of the message intended. For example, "If all your friends jumped off a cliff would you?" This message can be heard as, "You are not smart if you follow your friends' lead and/or your friends are stupid and/or family is smarter than friends." What is the reality for you? I have been in the position where my children and grandchildren at times have not had the smartest of friends, nor the best behaved, so I am guilty of saying that expression. The difference is that I followed it with a discussion of good decision making and taking time to reflect on the consequences of whatever action they were considering. I tried to instill the idea that they could be the good influence. For the most part, it worked.

Steve was told from a very early age that men didn't have fun that work was what made men happy. This belief was reinforced by what he saw his father doing which was working all the time. Even on family vacations Steve's dad took time to work. This belief was helpful while Steve was working, because it gave him a great work ethic and he realized a sense of accomplishment. When I asked Steve how this belief was working for him now, he replied, "Not too well." So Steve began to change his thinking to, "It is time for me to have fun with my family and friends. My work will be on my terms now."

Teresa and her husband completed this section of the workbook to determine from where her anxiety about moving and her friendships stemmed. Here it was simply that she had never moved before so her idea of friendship included being in close proximity. When she asked her friends about this belief some of them reminded her about their friends who had moved away but still stayed in touch.

A belief that I had about friendship was that if you had an argument with a friend, it would end the friendship. I believed that you had to be on the same page about everything to be friends. That belief came from my experiences as a small child. When I made a friend angry or disagreed with her, she was no longer willing to be my friend. This belief got in the way of being a good friend and of course keeping friendships. Annie taught me that even though I could make her angry, it was not the end of our friendship. We could work through it and still be friends. My belief system changed and changed for the better.

Let's pull apart some of the messages that are driving your behavior - the good and the bad. This is the first step in changing the message, and therefore, the behavior.

Write in the chart below the beliefs that you received about Social/Fun and the "hidden" message. Rate each message as positive or negative or both.

Take all the negative beliefs and re-write them or let them go.

Current Beliefs

Rewrite of Beliefs

For the next month, take note of occasions when a behavior gets in the way of your goals and track it back to a belief you might have received. Remind yourself of your rewritten belief, and soon the new belief, will drive improved behavior and get you to your goals.

Visualization

See yourself having fun. What does it look like? A great game of golf? Lying on the beach? Playing in the yard with the kids? Having a dinner party? Create your image of fun. Really get into it. Feel the movement, feel the sun, hear the ocean, hear the children laughing, hear your laughter.

See yourself with your friends. Feel their support during hard times. See them by your side on a walk. Hear their voices reminiscing over past experiences.

Picture yourself working with a community group to support a cause. Feel yourself walking or running in a 5K to support autism or cancer research. See the grateful faces of people you are helping through fundraising or serving food or some other function.

Positive Affirmation

I deserve to have fun with good and loyal friends.

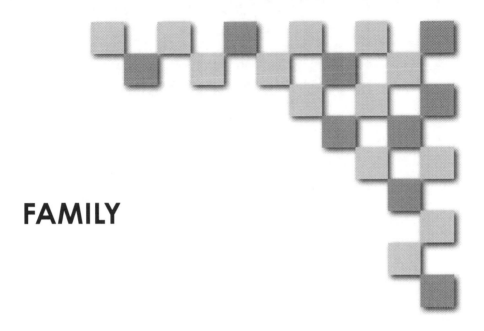

FAMILY

Family Rating

You can't exist in this life without a family. There was a mother and father at some point. If you do not have a biological family in your life, then use this section to look at your extended family. Who among your friends are really your family now? If there is no one, then work this chapter very hard. We all need family whether it is biological or spiritual.

Family usually gives you a significant safety net in life. We should trust family to take us in and protect us. It is family who knows us and forgives us and loves us just because we are – not because of anything superficial. I am referring here to a typical family with mostly healthy behaviors and traits (there is no family out there without some dysfunction!). If you drew the short straw and have a family that is dysfunctional to the point that they are damaging to you – you may want to keep them at a distance and get yourself some help so that you do not repeat their damaging behaviors.

We not only inherit biological and behavioral traits from our family, but also the environment where we grew up contributes to who we are. It is the nature and nurture issue. What is your family's story? What traits and behaviors can be tracked through the generations? Tempers? Depression? Optimism? Adventure? Don't be afraid to take a look and to ask questions. Get a good sense of what has been passed down to you and through you.

Linda's Big Move

Linda was going through a horrendous divorce. She and her two sons made the decision to move from their hometown to the town where her father and stepmother lived. This move was as brave as it was scary. Linda lived most of her life in her hometown and had believed that it was the best place to raise her children. But it was very expensive and housing was a significant problem. Another factor in her decision was that Linda's father offered her a position with his company that would lead to long-term success and security.

To make this move, Linda needed to find very inexpensive housing so that she could financially get on her feet again. It just so happened that her father lives in a five-bedroom home with three floors. Even though his mother-in-law was living with them, she was about eighty-years-old at the time and she had a bedroom on the second floor, he and his wife offered to let Linda and her boys live on the third floor with two bedrooms and their own bathroom to give her the chance to regroup after the divorce. She jumped at the offer. She and her children lived with her father, stepmother, and step-grandmother for a year and a half while she regrouped and got on her feet financially.

Such a huge offer and commitment usually comes only from family. She is now in her own home and her career is flourishing.

Not every family is capable of making such a generous offer and I don't want to position you for disappointment if you run and ask if you can move home, and the answer is no. So take a few minutes to think about what you believe your family would do for you if you were in need. This is important because if family coming to the rescue is Plan A in an emergency, and they can't or won't step up you had better have a Plan B in place.

Could they help you financially? How much? Are they there with emotional support? If you were sick and needed a kidney, would they step up and offer one to you? If their kidney wasn't a match would they organize a fundraiser and awareness rally to find one for you? It doesn't have to be so dramatic. What are your expectations of help with your children or pets? Can, or will, your family be there? You also have to ask: What are you willing to do for your family? Family is a two-way street; or, at least it should be one.

The Next Generation for Sam

Sam is the dealer principal and owner of a mid-sized material handling dealership in the Mid-west. He began the business as a start-up and it now has $75,000,000 in revenue. The issue is that Sam is getting older; he is now sixty-eight and he wants to retire. Sam has two children working in the business. His son, Bill, has been working in the business for seventeen years. Bill went to work for his father right after college with his degree in business management. Bill is currently the COO and is doing a decent job. Sam's daughter, Lauren, has been working in the business for the past eight years and is currently working in accounts receivable.

So, what is the problem? Sam has difficulty seeing his children as adults. He can't, or would prefer not to, let go of his role as father, teacher, and disciplinarian. Now it is getting in the way of his children taking over the business.

When Sam began this chapter he was surprised that even though his relationship with his immediate family is great, he was not letting go of his children to let them be independent. His rating here was a three and one-half, which many people would have left alone. Sam was not happy with his reason for not rating Family a five. He explored his beliefs about being a father. It became clear that he could retire and leave the business to the "kids" with a high level of trust. How did this happen?

Sam, began to give his children more responsibility and then stood back and let them perform. To his surprise, his children stepped up to the

85

responsibilities thrown at them and performed very well. Sam also asked the people around him what they thought of his children as managers and future owners. The answers were eye openers for Sam. Many said they trusted that his children would be great as the new owners. Some even said they thought Sam was a little behind the times and that his children were always bringing in new ideas and ways to do things.

Your Rating Regarding Family

Use the questions below to determine your rating on your family. Be realistic and be kind – they are your family.

- **Relationships** –
  o How are the relationships in your family?
  o Does everyone get along?
  o How are holidays? Tense? Fun?
  o Are you happy with the relationship you have with your family?
  o How is your relationship with your parents? Your children? Your siblings?
- **Trust** – Do you trust your family to tell the truth, to follow through, to back you up, to love you?
- **Support** – Is your family supportive or do they sabotage your efforts?
- **Extended Family** – Blended families are very common and if you are part of one, how are those relationships? These can be less important or more important to you. If there is an ex-spouse somewhere he or she could be stirring up lots of anxiety and tension. Stepchildren can be a blessing or a curse or something between.

What is your rating using the following scale:

1 – Dissatisfied - The worst.
2 – Somewhat dissatisfied - Need to make big changes.
3 – Satisfied - I need to make some changes.

4 – Somewhat satisfied - Just a tweak or two will make things better.

5 – Satisfied - No action is needed right now because I am happy with where things are.

I rate my family a _____

Reasons Regarding Family Rating

Write down the top three to five reasons you gave this area of your life the rating that you did. This is not only for negative reasons but also for positive reasons. For example, if you rated family a two you might site the following: I haven't spoken to my sister in two years. I have a good relationship with my adult children. Reasons have to be something that you can control. Then under each "reason", write down some steps you can take to improve, continue, or stop whatever the reason may be. Using our example from above "I haven't spoken to my sister in two years," you might write the following: I will begin contacting my sister through a letter. I will ask my mother to speak to my sister on my behalf.

Linda rated her Family section a four. Here were her reasons and goals with actions steps:

Reason: My dad is there for me, no matter what.
Goal: Keep the relationship strong
Action Steps:
-    Always interact with respect even when we disagree.
-    Spend time with dad and step-mom; have dinner, or just a coffee to talk.

Reason: I am very close to my children.
Goal: Make them independent people.
Action Steps:
-    Be friends with limits and structure.
-    Keep them accountable for their actions.
-    Have fun time with them. Lots of it!

Sam's rating of his Family as a three and one-half did not make him happy. He came up with many reasons why this Life Section was great but there was one area that brought the rating down. Let's look at the biggest reason Sam was very satisfied with this chapter on family and one area that brought his rating down.

Reason: I am close with my family. We not only love each other we like each other.
Goal: Maintain this closeness.
Action Steps:
- Make plans to spend time with my children outside of work.
- Have the grandchildren over at least every other week.
- Call my siblings monthly.

Reason: I don't believe my adult/children can take over the business.
Goal: Develop a more realistic assessment of my children.
Action Steps:
- Stop micro-managing them.
- Focus on the results they are getting not how they got there.
- Ask people who work with them for their honest opinion.

It is your turn now to fill in the blanks below with the reasons you rated this section as you did. This can be a more difficult section because it is about family. Be brave and write some action plans to increase your satisfaction with whatever kind of relationship you have with your family. There is a Life Section for your intimate partner so keep any reasons or actions having to do with your spouse or partner for that chapter.

Reason #1_____

_____

Goal:	Time Frame
Action Steps:	

Reason #2_____

_____

Goal:	Time Frame
Action Steps:	

Reason #3_____

_____

Goal:	Time Frame
Action Steps:	

Reason #4_____

_____

Goal:	Time Frame
Action Steps:	

Reason #5_____

_____

Goal:	Time Frame
Action Steps:	

Beliefs Regarding Family

What we have been told during our early years drives our adult behavior if we don't recognize and update these early beliefs. Sometimes we take the actual words of the message and put an implied meaning to it that may or may not be what the sender of the message intended; an example is, "Blood is thicker than water." This message can be imbedded as family first. The reality is that if you have a great family this works well, but not if you have a toxic family. In that case, putting them first may not be the best strategy for you to feel your best.

Let's pull apart some of the beliefs that are driving your behavior - the good and the bad. This is the first step in changing the belief and, therefore, the behavior.

Linda grew up hearing that family comes first, no matter what. When her father left her mother this belief led to a very strained relationship with her father for several years. She felt that even though the marriage was not healthy for him, he should have stayed because family comes first. When she identified that belief, she was able to alter it to a more mature belief, which was that her father's decisions were based on his life and his needs and that he did take into consideration everyone involved.

Sam believed that as the father, he was responsible for making all the decisions and for taking care of his children. He also believed that his children would always be children. So he believed that he had to micro-manage their lives to be a good dad. When he became cognizant of this belief, he actually laughed. He realized that it was not a healthy belief for himself or his kids—and it hindered his ability to retire. It took some time and effort but he changed that belief to: a dad's job is to help his kids become independent.

Write in the chart below the beliefs that you received about family. Take all the negative beliefs and rewrite them or let them go. A helpful hint here is to examine your family life when you were a kid. What was that like? What were the overriding messages/beliefs? Such as "Dad and Mom are always right"- "Don't question your parents, just do what they say." Both of these beliefs are great for small children to keep them safe and compliant, but do not work as the children grow up.

Current Beliefs

Rewrite of Beliefs

For the next month, take note of occasions when a behavior gets in the way of your goals and track it back to a message you might have received. Remind yourself of the re-write of that message and soon the new message will drive improved behavior and get you to your goals.

Visualization

Put together a photo album of your family in the best of times including weddings, birthdays, vacations, and such. It can be electronic or paper but keep it accessible. Look at these images fairly often to reinforce your good feelings toward your family.

Positive Affirmation

I accept my family as they are and love them unconditionally.

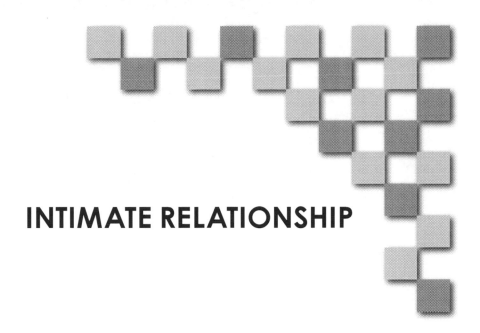

INTIMATE RELATIONSHIP

Intimate Relationship Rating

As we move into this chapter remember that no one is perfect in any of the roles that they have - not even you. As you rate your satisfaction with intimacy in your life, keep this in mind - no one is or can be the perfect person for you. This life area needs to be examined even if you do not have a special someone in your life such as a boyfriend or girlfriend, life partner, wife, or husband. Why? Because you may want someone in your life and you can use the information below to guide you in choosing that special someone. Or you may have decided that you want to live a solitary life but understand that having an intimate relationship (non-sexual) has many benefits. This relationship needs to be fostered and nurtured.

This chapter is not meant to be used to determine whether your current relationship is worth keeping. If you are having serious crises in your relationship, be smart and get help! This chapter is meant to assist you in making your current relationship stronger for both parties. It is meant to assist you in thinking through what you want in a relationship, if you are currently not in one. It also is meant to help you maintain a great relationship. Let's look at two examples.

My Story

I am very happy to be the successful relationship example. Bob and I met, worked together, fell in love, moved in with each other, and married - yes, in that order. Our relationship was not the first intimate relationship for either of us so we each had a set of luggage (baggage) that we brought into our union. That said, we also worked at unpacking that baggage and storing it in the attic or just throwing it away.

How? For one thing, we talked a lot! We helped each other sort through old beliefs and focus on what we had with each other. This process involved a lot of work, some tears (on my part) and lots of love and understanding. I did not want a repeat of my previous relationship. So I pulled apart what I

> **Intimacy is the capacity to be rather weird with someone - and finding that that's ok with them.**
>
> – Alain de Botton –

liked about my previous relationship, and what got in the way of keeping that relationship alive and healthy. I did not play the blame game and put all the responsibility on my ex-spouse. For example, I realized that I did not speak up for myself very well during my past marriage and that lead to built-up resentments. It also meant that I did not trust my ex to listen and take my needs and wants into consideration. This tactic does not leave my ex blameless but it focuses on what I can control and change which is a very powerful position indeed.

Every year when I complete Boom Life and come to this chapter, I work on it with Bob. We decide what is going well and then determine how to keep it going. We talk about what might need changing and we develop steps to remedy it.

For example, Bob and I travel a lot. Bob much more than I do. One year we decided that our time apart could become a problem and so we committed to never be apart for more than two weeks in a row and only once a year for that long a period. It has worked very well for us. As a matter of fact, I can only remember one time that we were apart for two weeks and we have been working together for twenty-eight years. That's not bad, in my opinion.

Bob and I really like to be together and so we commit to play together (some call this date night) at least once a week. When you work, live, and love with the same person, you can forget to have fun because you may begin to take for granted that they are there but that's not the same as quality time. So we do something just for us at least once a week. Talking is our sport and we are darn good at it and it is fun if the subject is fun. We dine out a lot and much more. This fun time keeps our spirits connected.

I attribute working this chapter together each year to being part of our success as a couple. We take a very pro-active approach to our relationship. We talk, set goals, and focus on us which keeps the relationship on track. It is fun, fulfilling, and fosters our love.

Fred and His Wife

Fred was in one of my leadership development classes (we use the Boom Life process in the classes) and at the end of the yearlong experience, he announced that for the first time in fifteen years of marriage his wife said that she would miss him when he left on his business trip. The class was very curious and asked for details.

Fred and his wife had a decent marriage, with three kids and a home they enjoyed. When Fred completed this chapter he began to realize that he had lost touch with the woman he married. Yes, they talked about the kids, the house, work, money, and more, but it was all very functional. He couldn't remember the last time he just looked her in the eye and asked how she was feeling. He decided to start asking.

The result was amazing to him. Such a simple change and his wife began to open up and talk about her dreams - for herself and for them as a couple. This actually allowed him to open up to her about what was rumbling around in his heart, too.

Their intimacy deepened and they looked forward to seeing each other for the first time in years. Fred also took this new habit and brought it to his relationships with his kids. He told us that listening without judgment or trying to fix things brought the family together.

He and his wife now complete this chapter yearly as a couple, and the family chapter as a family.

Your Rating of Intimate Relationship

It's your turn; use the questions below to help you determine your rating for intimate relationship.

- **Synergy**
  - o Are you better with this person in your life?
  - o Do the two of you make better decisions as a couple?
  - o Do you have goals in common?
  - o Do you both envision a future together?
- **Closeness**
  - o Do you feel accepted by the other person?
  - o Do you consider the other person a close friend as well as an intimate partner?
  - o Are you in love?
  - o Do you have fun together?
- **Physical Relationship** – This includes: hugs, kisses, handholding, sex, looks, etc.
- **Communication**
  - o Does communication take place?
  - o Is there understanding of the content and intent of what you say to each other?
- **Values**
  - o Are your values in line with each other? Respect, honesty, adventure, etc.

What is your rating using the following scale:

1 – Dissatisfied - The worst.
2 – Somewhat dissatisfied - Need to make big changes.
3 – Satisfied - I need to make some changes.
4 – Somewhat satisfied - Just a tweak or two will make things better.
5 – Satisfied - No action is needed right now because I am happy with where things are.

I rate my intimate relationship a _____

Reasons Regarding Intimate Relationship Rating

Write down the top three to five reasons you gave this area of your life the rating you did. This is not only for negative reasons but also for positive reasons.

For example, Bob and I rated Intimacy a five. We are very happy with our relationship yet, we want to be proactive about it, why? Here are some of our reasons.

Reason: We have separate identities and an identity as a couple.
Goal: Maintain some separate interests and continue our shared interests.
Action Steps:
- Give each other time and space for activities/hobbies away from each other.
- Respect the views and opinions of the other person even if different from the other.
- Continue our shared activities: sailing, movies, dining out, grandchildren, and so much more.

Reason: We like to spend time together.
Goal: Spend time together alone the days we are together.
Action Steps:
- Take a two-week vacation together every year that is non-work related.
- Talk with each other every day even if by phone.
- Date night once a week, even if we are away.

Fred gave his intimate relationship a three. He cited that he loved his wife. He trusted her. He didn't know her as well as he would like. He wanted to have more fun times with her. Fred committed to asking his wife what she was thinking and feeling, really listening to her, and opening up about his own feelings.

Reason: I've lost touch with my wife.
Goal: Get reacquainted with her.
Action Steps:
- Do more listening than talking.
- Be curious about her and ask for her opinions/thoughts/feelings.
- Spend time alone with her.

Reason: We are so focused on the kids that we don't have time for "us."
Goal: Spend time alone together.
Action Steps:
- Date night once a week.
- Dinner together whenever possible.
- Learn the art of conversation and bring in the entire family.

Reasons have to be something that you can control. Remember, you can't control your intimate partner, but by changing your normal routine he or she will have to adjust. Under each "reason" write down some steps you can take to improve, continue, or stop whatever the reason may be.

Reason #1_____

_____

Goal:	Time Frame
Action Steps:	

Reason #2_____

_____

Goal:	Time Frame
Action Steps:	

Reason #3_____

_____

Goal:	Time Frame
Action Steps:	

Reason #4_____

_____

Goal:	Time Frame
Action Steps:	

Reason #5_____

_____

Goal:		Time Frame
Action Steps:		

Beliefs Regarding Relationships

Write down in the chart below the beliefs that you received about relationships. For example, I grew up believing that a wife did all the listening and the husband did all the talking and decision making. I later found out that most of the discussion and decision making happened out of earshot of us kids. So it only looked as if dad was king. This outdated belief led me to keeping my thoughts to myself if I wasn't asked directly. I changed that belief to, "I need to speak my mind so that my partner knows my thoughts and opinions."

"A real man doesn't show his feelings," was a belief that Fred had internalized. This belief had him keeping his feelings to himself and his wife started keeping her feelings to herself. Eventually their conversations were only about their day-to-day lives. Fred changed his old belief to, "It is healthy to share and show my feelings." This new belief helped Fred with his commitment to get to know his wife again.

What are the messages about relationships that are embedded in your mind? How are your beliefs impacting your relationship? Decide which ones are still working for you and keep those. Take all the beliefs that are not working for you and re-write them or let them go.

Current Beliefs

Rewrite of Beliefs

Visualization

Imagine you and your partner sitting at a dinner enjoying the food, talking about life, goals, and opening up about hopes and fears. A feeling of trust and love surrounds both of you. Then, picture a perfect day with your partner. Where and how does it start? Where do you go? What do you do? Or maybe visualize that both of you are in agreement after a fun debate.

Another way is to remember one or two very happy times with your partner. Was it a nearly perfect vacation? A night at home during a storm where the conversation was intimate and you felt safe and connected? Or simply a night sitting on the sofa watching TV? Replay this over and over again. The results will be magic.

Positive Affirmation

I love my partner and enjoy being with him/her.

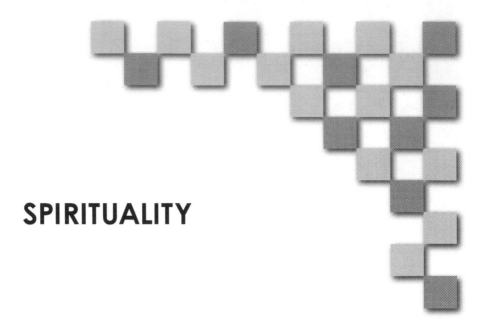

SPIRITUALITY

Spirituality Rating

We are all part of something much bigger than us. Your belief system is an important part of your life. Whether you are Christian, Muslim, Jewish, Hindu, Buddhist, Atheist, Secular Humanist, or whatever, taking the time to reflect, pray, or just be quiet is important for your wellbeing and growth as a person.

It is a very lucky person who can get through life without experiencing some major crisis or trauma. Think of those times your heart was broken, someone you loved ended up not loving you, you experience a physical trauma through an accident or illness, and other such times. Of course, we turn to those we love, our families, and partners, as well as friends, to help and support us through these times. For many, the knowledge that they are part of something much larger than themselves and that we are all connected through a higher power, provides a sense of comfort and hope.

Knowing that we are part of this Universal entity brings us together as one. It is why we take care of each other. It is why we love each other. It is why we connect in this physical world. It is because we are connected on a spiritual level.

Most religions have people gathering and praying together. Why? Because the sense of community, the sense of being part of a spiritual world provides comfort during sad times, strength during hard times, and increases our happiness during great times. Also, if you think of our thoughts, prayers, and petitions as energy then being part of a larger energy source provides greater results.

Many of you will realize that I am just touching the surface of a very profound and personal issue and you are right. I recommend asking those with more knowledge and expertise for more information. Read

> "Your sacred space is where you can find yourself over and over again."
> — Joseph Campbell

whatever sacred scripts you feel comfortable with and discuss the concepts, words, and meanings with other people.

Bill's Story

Bill started the Boom Life process because he felt that he could be happier or more satisfied with his life, but he couldn't put his finger on what was bothering him. He had scored high on six of the eight life areas: Health, Family, Social Fun, Environment, Career, and Finances. He scored somewhat lower on Intimate Relationship (he put some great action steps in force to correct this) and when he got to this chapter on Spirituality he was stumped. He scored this area a one!

This amazed him, because he was brought up in a religious family who attended services every week. He had also participated in church-organized volunteer efforts and had grown up saying his prayers every night. He wondered when all that had stopped. He realized that when he entered university and was on his own, he was at first relieved not to have to attend services. He really liked sleeping-in on Sundays. He found that he was only praying before a big test or when a paper was due. So when there was no stress, prayer did not happen.

After university, Bill went right to work at a large corporation and was putting in sixty-to sixty-five-hour weeks. He was on the fast track and his focus was on work. He met his wife at work (logical as that is where he was spending the majority of his time) and they married two years later. Both he and his wife are still focused on their careers and are extremely successful. But, Bill had that funny feeling in his stomach that he was missing the point about life.

As he contemplated his spirituality he realized that he had become very self-focused. He had lost sight of his connection with the world and especially God. He began by talking with his wife and they agreed to find a church that matched their belief system and where they felt comfortable. They began to attend services. Bill began to read the Bible and he began searching for opportunities to give back to others.

Bill's stress levels have come down significantly. He is much happier and even more satisfied with all the areas of his life. He is still successful, but he now shares his success with the less fortunate. Bill's journey back to his spirituality has made him more empathetic and, as a result, a better human being.

Petal's Story

Petal was born in the late seventies to free-thinking and free-living (hippie) parents. Her mom and dad never married and still live in the Greenwich Village apartment they had when Petal was born. Life with her parents was truly free and fun. Petal fondly remembers large groups of people coming and going from her home. There was music, dance, and lots of art which is how they made a living – creating jewelry.

Petal chose to complete Boom Life because she was not satisfied with her career (retail sales) or the income from her career. Most of her time was spent on those chapters with much success. It was when Petal came to this chapter on Spirituality that she furrowed her brow. Her first response was that she did not believe in God and so she could skip this chapter.

"Oh no, you don't," was my response. So Petal reflected on her spirituality. She had participated in many yoga retreats with her family and practiced yoga throughout her life. She soon realized that she thought of yoga as only a physical exercise. When the class would meditate or relax at the end of the session she would usually take stock of what she needed to get done after class.

Petal was able to recognize the spiritual philosophy that was handed down to her from her parents with the help of her current yoga teacher. This philosophy was more Eastern or Buddhist. Petal believed in the goodness of people. She lived an austere life and did not crave luxuries. She was put off by excesses in anything. She was a vegetarian. She always felt a part of a bigger source of energy and healing but never put a name to it. It was just there.

Her yoga teacher encouraged her to learn more about Buddha and the philosophy. Petal began to read and found a strong connection between herself and Buddhism. She began to learn to meditate. Her yoga experience deepened and she felt a sense of calm and confidence. Her ability to visualize changes that she wanted to make was strengthened. Petal's connection with the Universe put her at ease. She even found a Buddhist temple that offered the opportunity to meditate with a group and to discuss philosophy.

Petal admitted that this chapter influenced her life more than any other. Discovering her life philosophy (spirituality) opened her eyes to how she was living, what she believed, and brought about a sense of peace.

Take some time and reflect on your spirituality. If you grew up within a formal religion such as Catholic, Lutheran, Jewish, Muslim, or any of the other many religions, what do you still carry with you about your religion? Here are some doctrines to ponder.

Does the concept of a God conjure up the picture of an old man with a long beard, some bright orb pulsating in the sky, or the vision of all of us making up this entity called God? Whatever your vision, talk with God and ask God whatever you want; God will answer. As my father would say, "God talks to you all the time. Just know that God talks to you using your own voice." My dad was a wise man.

Were you taught the concepts of both prayer and meditation? If not, have you learned to meditate? If you currently pray or meditate, tap into the feelings that are initiated, such as hope, peacefulness, strength, gratitude, and the like. Science has shown that prayer and meditation, experienced on a regular basis, changes the brain and assists us in self-control, increasing our happiness, and sense of peace and more.

The questions to answer when determining your satisfaction with your spirituality are:

- Belief System
    o What do you believe in? God, Jesus, Buddha, Mohammed, or a Universal Energy that connects us all?
    o Do you spend time in contemplation of what you believe in terms of your part in the Universe?
    o Where do you turn when nothing on this physical earth seems to have the answer or help you need?
    o Do you trust in something greater than you and me?
- Religion
    o Do you practice a formal religion?
    o Do you get comfort and support from your religious dogma?
    o If your religion were outlawed tomorrow, what would your reaction be?
- Reflection
    o Do you take time to reflect, pray, or meditate? Whether it is walking in the woods, sitting on a beach…?
    o Have you had prayers/petitions answered more often than not?

    o   Do you feel as though you need to be in control all the time?
- Can you let go and believe?
  - o   Do you share your success/wealth/knowledge with those less fortunate from you out of a sense of connection?

What is your rating using the following scale:

1 – Dissatisfied - The worst.
2 – Somewhat dissatisfied - Need to make big changes.
3 – Satisfied - I need to make some changes.
4 – Somewhat satisfied - Just a tweak or two will make things better.
5 – Satisfied - No action is needed right now because I am happy with where things are.

I rate my spirituality a _____

Reasons Regarding Spirituality Rating

Bill had rated his spirituality a one his first time through Boom Life. His top two reasons are here:

Reason: I haven't practiced my religion in many years.
Goal: Reconnect with my faith.
Action Steps:
- Find a church to attend.
- Pray daily.
- Read spiritual material.

Reason: I find myself very self-absorbed.
Goal: Become more aware and involved with the world around me.
Action Steps:
- Volunteer at a charitable organization such as the local soup kitchen.
- Financially contribute to a few non-profit organizations.
- Get involved with mission work at the church.

Petal ended up enjoying this chapter quite a bit. Her first pass at rating her Spirituality was a two. Here are some of her reasons.

Reason: I practice yoga.
Goal: Learn more of the spiritual side of yoga.
Action Steps:
- Pay attention during yoga class to the meditation/relaxation part.
- Read more about Buddha.

Reason: I don't know what I believe.
Goal: Discover what it is I believe about God, Universe, or whatever.
Action Steps:
- Read several books on different religions and philosophies.
- Attend different services.
- Ask my friends what they believe and why.

It's now your turn to write down the top three to five reasons why you gave this area of your life the rating that you did. This is not only for negative reasons but also for positive reasons. If you rated your spirituality a four you might site the following: I am Christian; I pray every day; I trust in God; I would like to find a church to attend. Then under each reason write down some steps you can take to improve, continue, or stop whatever the reason may be. Using our example from above, "I would like to find a church to attend," you might write the following: I will visit a different church every week for two months. I will ask friends where they attend services.

Reason #1_____

_____

Goal:	Time Frame
Action Steps:	

Reason #2_____

_____

Goal:	Time Frame
Action Steps:	

Reason #3_____

_____

Goal:	Time Frame
Action Steps:	

Reason #4_____

_____

Goal:	Time Frame
Action Steps:	

Reason #5_____

_____

Goal:		Time Frame
Action Steps:		

Beliefs Regarding Spirituality

This section might be a little tricky because it is all about beliefs. Which beliefs am I talking about here? Well, you need to examine the beliefs you have about your beliefs. Okay, that was confusing so let's look at Bill's beliefs. He realized that one of his beliefs was that you only needed to pray when you needed something. This belief came from his youth when every prayer he said seemed to be asking for something such as good health, or, care for his family. He realized that when he became a college student and wanted to do things for himself that his belief that you only pray when you need something stopped him from continuing to pray because he wanted to do things himself. He rewrote that belief to say, "I believe that prayer is a dialogue with God and it includes gratitude as well as petitions."

Petal found that one of her stronger beliefs was that it didn't matter what you believed - anything goes. This belief prevented her from really thinking about her belief system. She changed that belief to be, "It is important to define your beliefs in God or the Universal energy so that you can connect and be at peace."

Write down the beliefs that you received about spirituality/religion in the chart below, and the "hidden" messages. Some of us received the direct message that if we didn't follow our religion we would go to hell. It is scary to think that even our rational minds can still hear this old message and send guilt our way.

Rate each message as positive or negative, or both. Take all the negative beliefs and rewrite them or let them go.

Current Beliefs
Rewrite of Beliefs

Visualization

Feel the peace that comes from believing that you are part of a power greater than any individual and that this power has the ability to take care of your needs by showing you the way.

Imagine relinquishing all your worries and challenges to God to take care of for you. What a relief.

Feel the strength and hope in the embrace of whatever Universal energy you believe.

Positive Affirmation

I invite the divine to enter my life through prayer, meditation, or communion with nature.

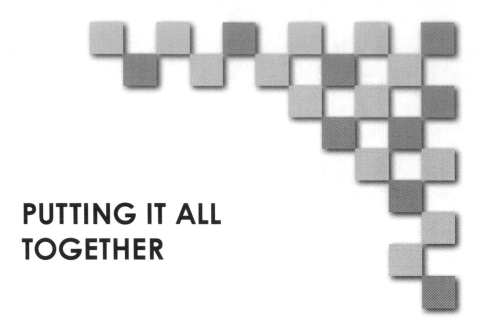

PUTTING IT ALL TOGETHER

Congratulations! You got through the workbook; or did you skip around and just land here at the last chapter to see what I would have to say at this point? Whatever your answer is, welcome to the last chapter where you can review, prioritize, and get going.

At this point, I hope that you have experienced success in one or more of the life areas due to working the Boom Life process and are motivated to continue this journey.

Michael had been working Boom Life for a few years when he suffered a major heart attack. He was only fifty-two and still working. He called me, and told me that if this had happened to him without his going through Boom Life his anxiety would have been extreme.

Because of his planning and focus on enhancing his life he was able to:

- put his career on hold for a few months without fear of losing any forward momentum;

- lean on his family and friends for support at home such as mowing the lawn;
- be confident that his finances were in order and that they could handle this crisis; and
- know that his wife, children, grandchildren, and friends knew that he loved them without any doubt.

Michael recovered from his heart attack quicker than the doctors expected. He is back at work, play, and life with even more gusto than before.

So now let's get human! No matter how you went through this workbook - filled out every exercise as you went along or just read through and will go back to one or two life areas at a time - you might be wondering where you get the motivation to stick to whatever action plans you choose to focus on first.

I wish I had "the" answer for you, but unfortunately each of you reading this book will have to find your own motivation to stick to your plans. It will be easier for some, but everyone needs to think this through. Here are some ideas to help you in this area.

The number-one strategy to keep on plan is to get other people involved in the plan. This creates accountability. After my second divorce, when I started to focus on who I was dating and what I was looking for in an intimate partner, I recruited my best friend, Annie, who would help me evaluate how well the person I was dating fit my new criteria. She was tough and didn't let me off the hook. I figured out I was looking in the wrong "frog pond" and had to move along so that I could attract a different breed of frog. It worked!

Let's look at some of the common support systems.

- Family is a big support system for many. Your love partner, parents, siblings, and adult children are important people in your life and if possible, will support you through your changes. Think of who you can trust in your family to have your back. Include people in your change initiatives. Ask them to help if they can, or to just listen.

- Friends in today's world can be an important part of your support. Many people develop a strong, close set of friends to support them in their lives. It is critical to make sure that your friends have similar values to yours. If you have friends with conflicting values you will find them moving you toward their own value system.
- Co-workers can be a great support, especially in the area of career. Americans spend the majority of their time at work and so develop strong relationships with their co-workers. Ask a trusted co-worker for their advice, or to just listen to your goals is wonderful.
- Organizations such as Weight Watchers, churches, spiritual centers, and clubs can offer you support in achieving more satisfaction in a specific life area, based on the organization.
- Professionals are a great source of support. You may want to include personal trainers, life coaches, doctors, lawyers, counselors, and others that will provide you with accountability.

Review of Mission Statement

Now that you have finished each of the chapters, it is time to go back and review your Mission Statement. Are you remaining true to your Mission? Has your work on Boom Life illuminated a need to modify your Mission Statement? If yes, then do so here.

_____

_____

_____

_____

Prioritizing Goals

Now that you have either reinforced your Mission or modified it, this step will assist you in prioritizing all the action steps that you have identified.

1. Arrange the Life Areas in order of importance from highest to lowest.
2. Under each area, prioritize the improvement steps you have identified.
3. Continue to set aside time to review your progress.
4. Continue to relax and visualize your Boom Life daily.

Visualizations and Positive Affirmations

Review and continue to use the visualizations and positive affirmations at the end of each chapter. The more focused and relaxed you are the more easily and quickly change takes place. Which visualization and positive affirmation were your favorites? Repeat them every day.

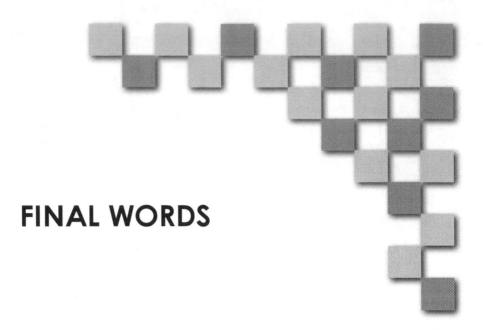

FINAL WORDS

You have begun the process of enhancing your life. Do not stop. I had been in therapy for several years before I finally filed for my second divorce. One of my children had been acting out and I was concerned. The psychologist said to me that before I could help my child I had to help myself. I think I cried for days over that piece of advice. I just wanted my child to be better; I would help her, but what did it have to do with me?

I stopped crying and bit my trembling lower lip and went into therapy. Right, not my child but me, not my husband but me, I started the process thinking I was to blame. That was way back in 1987. I stayed in therapy until 1991.

Here is what I learned:

I played a part in the family drama but I was not to "blame."
I learned assertiveness - to speak up.
I learned what triggered my feelings - what made me "tick."
I learned to understand my actions and reactions and then to modify them for better results.
I learned that as painful as self-awareness can be, it is worth it.
I learned to love myself.

I learned that when I changed myself, everyone around me had to change too. They had to react differently when I changed.

I learned who I was, and why I was who I was, and that I was okay.

I learned to change my behavior through changing my thoughts and beliefs.

I found that as I changed, my child also changed. My other children became stronger. My husband and I had a very civil divorce. I was finally in control of me and, therefore, my life. I still needed a structure to help me tackle my life on a recurring basis and so Boom Life came alive.

I took this lesson and superimposed it on every area of my life. What was I doing in terms of my finances, family relationships, health, environment, career, intimate relationship, spirituality, fun and friends? I was the pivotal point. I was capable of making changes that would enhance my life. It was up to me.

Believe me when I say that life is never perfect. We lose people we love. My parents have passed as well as one of my brothers and many other people I have loved. We see people we care about struggle with their demons. Addiction is no stranger to my family. We see people fail and make life-altering mistakes. We must learn to cope with these challenges through support and spirituality. I have learned to live from the inside out.

Like me, you might have picked up this book because you want something in your life to get better and you had hoped that the answer to get someone else or some situation to change would be here. Sorry, that will not happen. You are the change that needs to happen. You can do it. Take it in steps.

Use the cognitive behavioral connection, it works, if you work it, so work it, because you're worth it (borrowed from NarAnon). Think of physical exercise. You have to do the exercises in order to get the benefits. You can't do fifty sit ups and think that you will have six pack abs. You must do them consistently and over a long period of time. Re-training your brain and thoughts is the same. Just doing it once will not reap long lasting benefits. You must do it over and over again for a long period of time. You can do it. Like exercise, you become used to it and miss it if you skip a day or two.

Create a better future for yourself by first envisioning it. What does it look like? Create a dream board for yourself with pictures of what you are striving for such as; the job you want, the house you dream about, pictures of your family having fun, and the dream vacation.

A friend of ours has a dream board and she puts all sorts of wonderful things on it. She is a businesswoman who makes jewelry and she had a picture of O, Oprah's magazine, on the board. She could see her jewelry being part of that magazine and indeed after three years on that board, her jewelry was part of an article on clothing and accessories in the magazine. She had to do her part by frequently submitting her jewelry for their consideration.

Always remember the story of the young man who prayed to God to let him win the lottery. He prayed and prayed and prayed. After twenty years of not winning, the man was angry and asked God why he hadn't won the lottery yet. God finally spoke to him and said, "You have to do your part. Now go out and buy a ticket."

That is what this workbook is all about: not only dreaming but designing the steps to enhance your life.

So, dream big and create a Boom Life for yourself.

Printed in the United States
By Bookmasters